Jean-Baptiste Arban

Célèbre méthode complète de trompette cornet à piston et saxhorn

Volume 1

Jean-Baptiste Arban

Célèbre méthode complète de trompette cornet à piston et saxhorn

Volume 1

ISBN/EAN: 9783956980879

Auflage: 1

Erscheinungsjahr: 2014

Erscheinungsort: Norderstedt, Deutschland

Hergestellt in Europa, USA, Kanada, Australien, Japan
Europäischer Musikverlag in Hansebooks GmbH, Norderstedt

A LIST OF THE PRINCIPAL WORDS USED IN MODERN MUSIC.

WITH THEIR ABBREVIATIONS AND EXPLANATIONS.

A .... to, in, or at; *A tempo*, in time.
Accelerando (accel.) ..... Gradually increasing the speed.
Accent .... Emphasis on certain parts of the measure.
Adagio .... Slow; leisurely.
Ad libitum (ad lib.) .... At pleasure; not in strict time.
A due (a 2) .... To be played by both instruments.
Agitato .... Restless, with agitation.
Al or *Alla* .... In the style of.
Alla Marcia .... In the style of a March.
Allegretto .... Moderately quick.
Allegro .... Quick and lively.
Allegro assai .... Very rapidly.
Amore .... Love. *Con amore*, Fondly; tenderly.
Amoroso .... Affectionately.
Andante .... In moderately-slow time.
Andantino .... A little less slow than Andante.
Anima, con } With animation.
Animato }
A piacere .... At pleasure.
Appassionato .... Impassioned.
Arpeggio .... A broken chord.
Assai .... Very: *Allegro assai*, very rapidly.
A tempo .... In the original movement.
Attacca .... Commence the next movement at once.
Barcarolle .... A Venetian boatman's song.
Ben .... Well; *Ben marcato*, well marked.
Bis .... Twice; repeat the passage.
Bravura .... Brilliant, bold, spirited.
Brillante .... Showy, sparkling, brilliant.
Brio, con .... With much spirit.
Cadenza .... A passage introduced as an embellishment.
Calando .... Decreasing in power and speed.
Cantabile .... In a singing style.
Caprice .... A composition of irregular construction.
Capriccio, a .... At pleasure.
Cavatina .... A movement in vocal style. [sounds.
Chord .... A combination of three or more musical
Coda .... A finishing movement.
Col or *con* .... With.
Crescendo (cres.) .... Gradually louder.
Da or *dal* .... From.
Da Capo (D. C.) ...... From the beginning.
Dal Segno (D. S.) .... From the sign.
Decrescendo (decresc.) .Decreasing in strength.
Delicatezza, con ..... Delicately; refined in style.
Diminuendo (dim.) .... Gradually softer.
Divisi .... Divided. Each part to be played by a sepa-
Dolce .... Softly, sweetly. [rate instrument.
Dolcissimo .... Very sweetly and softly.
Dominant .... The fifth tone in the major or minor scale.
Duet or *duo* .... A composition for two performers.
E .... And.
Elegante .... Elegant; graceful.
Embouchure .... The mouthpiece of a wind instrument.
Enharmonic .... Alike in pitch but different in notation.
Energico .... With energy, vigorously.
Espressione, con ..... Expressively, with expression.
Finale .... The concluding movement.
Fine .... The end.
Forte (f) .... Loud.
Forte-piano (fp) ..... Loud and instantly soft again.
Fortissimo (ff) ...... Very loud.
Forza .... Force of tone.
Forzando (fz) .... Accentuate the sound.
Fuoco, con .... With fire; with spirit.
Furioso .... Furiously; passionately.
Giocoso .... Joyously; playfully.
Giusto .... Exact; in strict time.
Grandioso .... Grand; pompous; majestic.
Grave .... Very slow and solemn.
Grazioso .... Gracefully.
Gusto .... Taste.
Harmony .... A combination of musical sounds.
Key-note .... The first degree of the Scale.
Largamente .... Very broad in style.
Larghetto .... Slow, but not so slow as Largo.
Largo .... Broad and slow.
Legato .... Smoothly, the reverse of Staccato.
Leger-line .... A small added line above or below the staff.
Leggiero .... Lightly.
Lento .... Slow, but not as slow as Largo.
L'istesso tempo ...... In the same time.
Loco .... Play as written, no longer 8va.
Ma .... But. *Ma non troppo*, But not too much.
Maestoso .... Majestically, dignified.
Maggiore .... Major Key.
Marcato .... Marked. With distinctness and emphasis.

Meno .... Less. *Meno mosso*, Less quickly.
Mezzo .... Moderately.
Mezzo piano (mp) .... Moderately soft.
Minore .... Minor Key.
Moderato .... Moderately. *Allegro moderato*, moderately
Molto .... Much; very. [fast.
Morendo .... Gradually softer.
Mosso .... Moved. *Piu mosso*, quicker.
Moto .... Motion. *Con moto*, with animation.
Non .... Not.
Notation .... { The art of representing musical sounds
                         { by characters visible to the eye.
Obligato .... An indispensable part.
Octave .... A series of 8 consecutive diatonic tones.
Opus (Op.) .... A work.
Ossia .... Or; or else. Generally indicating an easier
Ottava (8va) .... To be played an octave higher. [method.
Pause (⌒) .... The sign indicating pause or finish.
Perdendosi .... Dying away gradually.
Pesante .... Heavily; with firm and vigorous execution.
Piacere, a .... At pleasure.
Pianissimo (pp) ..... Very soft.
Piano (p) .... Soft.
Piu .... More. *Piu Allegro*, More quickly.
Poco or *un poco* ... A little.
Poco a poco .... Gradually, by degrees.
Poco piu mosso .... A little faster.
Poco meno .... A little slower.
Poco piu .... A little faster.
Poi .... Then; afterwards.
Pomposo .... Pompous; grand.
Prestissimo .... As fast as possible.
Presto .... Very quick; faster than Allegro.
Primo (1mo) .... The first.
Quartet .... A piece of music for four performers.
Quasi .... As if; similar to; in the style of.
Quintet .... A piece of music for five performers.
Rallentando (rall.) . Gradually slower.
Rinforzando .... With special emphasis.
Rilardando (rit.) ... Slackening speed.
Risoluto .... Resolutely; bold; energetic.
Ritenuto .... Retarding the time.
Scherzando .... Playfully, sportively.
Secondo (2do) .... The second time (or part.)
Seconda volta .... The second time.
Segue .... Follow on in similar style.
Semplice .... Simply; unaffectedly.
Sempre .... Always; continually.
Senza .... Without. *Senza sordino*, Without mute.
Sforzando (sf) ...... Forcibly; with sudden emphasis.
Simile .... In like manner.
Smorzando (smorz.) .. Diminishing the sound.
Solo .... For one performer only.
Sordino .... A Mute. *Con Sordino*, With the Mute.
Sostenuto .... Sustained, prolonged.
Sotto .... Under. *Sotto voce*, In a subdued tone.
Spirito .... Spirit. *Con Spirito*, Forcefully.
Staccato .... Detached, separated.
Stentando .... Dragging or retarding the tempo.
Stretto .... An increase of speed. *Piu Stretto*, Faster.
Subdominant .... The 4th tone in the diatonic scale.
Syncopation .... Change of accent from a strong beat to a
Tacet .... Be silent. [weak one.
Tempo .... Movement.
Tempo primo .... As at first.
Tenuto (ten.) .... Held for the full value.
Theme .... The subject or melody.
Timbre .... Quality of tone.
Tonic .... The key-note of any scale.
Tremolo .... A trembling, fluttering movement.
Trio .... A piece of music for three performers.
Triplet .... { A group of 3 notes to be performed in the
                         { time of two of equal value.
Troppo .... Too much. *Allegro ma non troppo*, not too
Tutti .... All; all the instruments. [quick.
Un .... A; one; an.
Unison .... Alike in pitch.
Una corda .... On one string.
Variation .... The transformation and embellishment of a
Veloce .... Rapid; swift; quick. [melody.
Vibrato .... A wavy tone-effect which should be sparing-
Vivace .... With vivacity; bright; spirited. [ly used.
Vivo .... Lively.
Voce .... The voice; a certain part.
Volkslied .... A national or folk song.
Volti subito (V. S.) . Turn over quickly.

REPORT

of the Conservatory's Committee on Music Study regarding Mr. Arban's Cornet Method.

The Committee on Music Study has examined and tested the Method submitted to them by Mr. Arban.

This work is rich in instructive advice, is based upon the best of fundamental principles, and omits not a single instructive point which might be needed for the development and gradual technical perfection of a player.

The work might be classed as a general resumé of the ability and knowledge acquired by the author during his long experience as a teacher of and performer upon his instrument, and in a certain sense embodies the remarkable results achieved by him during his long career as a soloist.

Every variety of articulation, tonguing, staccati, etc., is thoroughly treated, ingeniously analyzed and clearly explained. The plentiful exercising material provided for each of these various difficulties is deserving of particular mention. Instructive points touching upon all possible musical questions are treated at length and throughout the work we have observed a profound appreciation of all difficulties and masterly ability to overcome them on the part of the author. The latter part of the work contains a long succession of studies, as interesting in subject as in form, and concludes with a collection of solos, which are, as it were, the embodiment or application of the previous lessons. These studies and solos give plentiful evidences of all those brilliant and thorough qualifications of which the author has so often given proof in his public performances.

In consequence the committee feels no hesitation in expressing its appreciation and approval of Mr. Arban's Method and recommends that same be adopted unreservedly for instruction at the Conservatory.

BERICHT

des Comités des Conservatoriums für musikalische Studien über die Cornet à Pistons-Schule des Herrn Arban.

Das Comité für musikalische Studien hat die Methode geprüft, welche ihm Herr Arban unterbreitet hat.

Dieses Werk enthält reichliche Aufklärungen, beruht auf ausgezeichneten Lehrsätzen und lässt keine Belehrungen bei Seite, die geeignet sind, einen guten Cornettisten zu bilden.

Es ist gewissermassen das Résumé der vom Verfasser erlangten Kenntnisse, die er in einer langen Praxis als Lehrer und ausübender Künstler gewonnen, und eine schriftliche Besiegelung der ausserordentlichen Resultate, die seine Carrière als Virtuos bezeichnen.

Die verschiedenen Arten der Articulation, des Zungenstosses, die Verzierungsnoten, die *Staccati*, sind gründlich abgehandelt, geistreich analysirt und glücklich gelöst. Die zahlreichen Lectionen, die ihnen der Autor widmet, haben ein Recht auf ganz besondere Erwähnung.

In der reichen Folge von Belehrungen, in denen auch alle sonstigen musikalischen Fragen behandelt sind, bemerkt man gleichzeitig eine ebenso tiefe Einsicht in die Schwierigkeiten als einen vollendeten Takt, ihrer Herr zu werden. Der letzte Theil des Werkes enthält eine lange Reihe von Etuden, ebenso interessant durch ihren Inhalt als durch ihre Form, und schliesst mit der Sammlung von Solostücken, die die practische Anwendung dessen, was vorher gelehrt wurde, enthalten. Aus diesen Etuden und Solos leuchten alle die glänzenden und soliden Eigenschaften hervor, von denen der Verfasser so oft Proben gegeben hat.

In Folge dessen steht das Comité nicht an, in gerechter Anerkennung des Verdienstes und der Nützlichkeit der Methode, deren Autor Herr Arban ist, dieselbe für den Unterricht im Conservatorium einzuführen.

RAPPORT

du Comité des Études musicales du Conservatoire, sur la Méthode de Cornet à pistons et de Saxhorn de M. Arban.

Le Comité des études musicales a examiné la Méthode qui lui a été soumise par M. Arban.

Cet ouvrage, comportant des développements considérables, repose sur d'excellentes doctrines et n'omet aucun des enseignements propres à former un bon cornettiste.

C'est, en quelque sorte, le résumé des connaissances acquises par l'auteur, au moyen d'une longue pratique comme professeur et exécutant, et une consécration écrite des résultats exceptionnels dont a été marquée sa carrière de virtuose.

Les différents genres d'articulations, les divers coups de langue, les notes d'agrément, les *staccati* sont sérieusement abordés, ingénieusement analysés et heureusement résolus; les nombreuses leçons qu'y consacre l'auteur ont droit à une mention toute particulière.

Dans la riche série d'enseignements où sont traitées toutes les autres question musicales, on remarque également une intelligence approfondie des difficultés et un tact parfait à en triompher. La dernière partie de l'ouvrage renferme une longue suite d'études aussi intéressantes par le fond que par la forme, et se termine par une collection de solos qui sont comme la mise en œuvre de ce qui a été enseigné précédemment: dans ces études et dans ces solos brillent les qualités éclatantes et solides à la fois dont l'auteur a si souvent fait preuve.

En conséquence, le Comité, rendant hommage au mérite et à l'utilité de la Méthode dont M. Arban est l'auteur, n'hésite pas à l'approuver, ainsi qu'à l'adopter pour l'enseignement au Conservatoire.

AUBER, MEYERBEER, KASTNER, A. THOMAS,
REBER, BAZIN, BENOIST, DAUVERNÉ, VOGT, PRUMIER, EMILE PERRIN,
EDOUARD MONNAIS,   A. DE BEAUCHESNE,
Imperial Commissioner.   *Secretary.*

Biographical Sketch of Joseph-Jean-Baptiste-Laurent Arban.

This illustrious artist was born at Lyons, France, February 28, 1825. He entered the Conservatory at an early age, taking up the study of the trumpet under Dauverne, and won first prize in 1845. His military term was passed in the navy on board the "La Belle Poule," whose chief musician, Paulus became Chief Musician of the Garde à Paris during the reign of Napoleon III.

After having been professor of Saxhorn at the Military school (1857), he was elected professor of Cornet at the Conservatory January 23, 1869. After attending to these duties for a term of five years, Arban left the Conservatory for six years, returning again in 1880.

He was the most brilliant cornet player of his time, and his astonishing performances and triumphant concert tours throughout Europe were the means of establishing the Valve Cornet as one of the most popular of all musical instruments. Arban's artistic ideals, sound musicianship and invaluable instructive principles were perpetuated in his splendid "Method for the Cornet," which has succeeded in maintaining the very highest position among similar instructive works and which has never been surpassed in point of practical superiority or artistic plan.

Arban died at Paris on April 9, 1889. He was an officer of the Academie, Knight of the Order of Leopold of Belgium, of Christ of Portugal, and of Isabella the Catholic, and of the Cross of Russia.

Joseph-Jean-Baptiste-Laurent Arban.
Biographische Skizze.

Dieser berühmte Künstler sah in Lyons, Frankreich, am 28-ten Feb. 1825, das Licht der Welt. In jugendlichen Alter trat er in das Konservatorium ein, um unter Dauverne Unterricht auf der Trompete zu nehmen, und in Jahre 1845 gewann er den ersten Preis. Seine Dienstzeit absolvirte er bei der Marine an Bord der "La Belle Poule," deren Kapellmeister, Paulus, Kapellmeister der Garde à Paris wurde wärend der Regierung Napoleons III.

Nachdem er an der Militär Schule Lehrer für Saxhorn gewesen (1857), wurde er zum Cornet Lehrer gewählt am Konservatorium, am 23-ten Januar, 1869. Nachdem er sich dieser Thätigkeit fünf Jahre lang gewidmet hatte, verliess Arban das Konservatorium auf sechs Jahre, im Jahre 1880 dorthin zurück-kehrend.

Er war der hervorragendste Cornettist seiner Zeit, und seine erstaunliche Fertigkeit, sowie seine Triumphe auf allen Konzertbühnen Europas, machten das Cornet à Pistons bald zu einem der beliebtesten aller Musik Instrumente. Arban's künstlerisches Ideal, seine musikalische Tüchtigkeit und seine unvergleichlichen Lehrgrundsätze, wurden verewigt in seiner ausgezeichneten Cornet-Methode, welche noch immer den ersten Platz unter derartigen Werken für Lehrzwecke behauptet, und noch nie übertroffen worden ist, was praktischen Wert und künstlerische Anlage betrifft.

Arban starb in Paris am 9-ten April, 1889. Er war Mitglied der Akademie, Ritter des belgischen Leopold Ordens, des Christi von Portugal, des Katholischen Isabellen Ordens und des russischen Kreuzes.

Trait Biographique de la vie de Joseph-Jean-Baptiste-Laurent Arban.

Ce célèbre musicien est né a Lyon, en France, le 28-me Fevrier, 1825. Il fut élève du Conservatoire encore jeune, pour étudier la trompette sous Daverné, et obtint le premier prix en 1845. Son devoir militaire fut passé dans la marine sur "La Belle Poule" donc le chef de musique, Paulus, devint chef de musique de la Garde à Paris pendant le reigne de Napoleon III.

Après avoir été professeur de la classe de saxhorn a l'école militaire (1857) il fut nommé professeur d'une classe de cornet au Conservatoire le 23-me Janvier, 1869. Après qu'il s'était devoué à ces devoirs pendant une période de cinque ans, Arban quitta le Conservatoire pour six ans, retournant de nouveau en 1880.

Il était le plus brillant cornettiste de son jour et son jeu étonnant, ainsi que les triomphes que lui accordait toute l'Europe pendant ses tournées de concerts, furent le moyen d'etablir le cornet à pistons comme un des plus populaires d'instruments musicals. Arban a perpetué son ideal d'Art, son profond savoir musical, et ses remarquables principes instructifs dans son excellente Methode pour le Cornet qui retient encore le premier rang parmi les oeuvres instructifs de mêne genre, et n'a jamais été surpassée au point de superiorité pratique ou de plan artistique.

Arban mourut a Paris le 9-me Avril, 1889. Il était un officier de l'Académie, Chevalier de l'Ordre de Leopold de Belge, de Christ de Portugal, d'Isabelle la Catholique, et de la Croix Russe.

PREFACE.

It may appear somewhat strange to undertake the defense of the cornet at a time when this instrument has given proofs of its excellence, both in the orchestra and in solo performances, where it is no less indispensable to the composer, and not less liked by the public than the flute, the clarinet, and even the violin; where, in short, it has definitely won for itself the elevated position to which the beauty of its tone, the perfection of its mechanism and the immensity of its resources, so justly entitle it.

But this was not always the case; the cornet was far less successful when it first appeared; and, indeed, not many years ago, the masses treated the instrument with supreme indifference, while that time-honored antagonist — routine — contested its qualities, and strove hard to prohibit their application. This phenomenon, however, is of never-failing recurrence at the birth of every new invention, however excellent it may be, and of this fact the appearance of the saxhorn and the saxophone, instruments of still more recent date than the cornet, gave a new and striking proof.

The first musicians who played the cornet were, for the most part, either horn or trumpet players. Each imparted to his performance the peculiarities resulting from his tastes, his abilities and his habits, and I need scarcely add that the kind of execution which resulted from so many incomplete and heterogeneous elements was deficient in the extreme, and, for a long while, presented the lamentable spectacle of imperfections and failures of the most painful description.

Gradually, however, matters assumed a more favorable aspect. Executants, really worthy of the name of artists, began to make their appearance. However, regardless of the brilliant accomplishments of such performers, they could not deny the faults of their original training, viz., the total lack of qualifications necessary for ensemble playing, and decided musicianly tendencies. Some excited admiration for their extreme agility; others were applauded for the expression with which they played; one was remarkable for lip; another for the high tone to which he ascended; others for the brilliancy and volume of their tone. In my opinion, it was the reign of specialists, but it does not appear that a single one of the players then in vogue ever thought of realizing or of obtaining the sum total of qualities which alone can constitute a great artist.

This, then, is the point upon which I wish to insist, and to which I wish to call particular attention. At the present time, the incompleteness of the old school of performers is unanimously acknowledged, as is also the insufficiency of their instruction. That which is required is methodical execution and methodical instruction. It is not sufficient to phrase well or to execute difficult passages with skill. It is necessary that both these things should be equally well done.

VORREDE.

Es könnte sonderbar oder überflüssig erscheinen, heut zu Tage ein Wort zur Vertheidigung des Cornet à Pistons zu verlieren, wo dieses Instrument seine Proben im Orchester und Solo bestanden, wo es dem Componisten ebenso unentbehrlich und vom Publicum ebenso geschätzt ist, als die Flöte, die Clarinette und selbst die Violine, heut, wo es sich entschieden denjenigen Rang erobert hat, den ihm die Schönheit seines Klanges, die Vollendung seines Mechanismus und die Unermesslichkeit seiner Hülfsquellen anweisen.

Aber es ist nicht immer so gewesen. Das Cornet hat bescheidenere Anfänge gehabt, und es ist noch nicht viele Jahre her, dass man es allgemein mit stolzer Gleichgültigkeit aufnahm und zu gleicher Zeit die heilige Phalanx der Routine seine guten Eigenschaften bestritt und sich Mühe gab seine Anwendung zu proscribiren, eine Erscheinung, welche übrigens bei keiner neuen Erfindung sich zu zeigen verfehlt, mag diese auch noch so ausgezeichnet sein, und von der das Auftauchen des Saxhornes und Saxophons, jüngere Instrumente als das Cornet, neue und eclatante Beweise geliefert hat.

Die ersten Musiker, welche das Cornet à Pistons bliesen, waren in der Regel Hornisten oder Trompeter. Jeder that die Eigenthümlichkeit seines Geschmacks, seiner Fähigkeiten und Gewohnheiten hinzu, und ich brauche nicht zu bemerken, dass eine Execution, die aus so viel unvollkommenen und fremdartigen Elementen entstand, lange Zeit zu wünschen übrig liess, und ebenso lange das traurige Schauspiel der verletzendsten Lücken, Unvollkommenheiten und Fehler darbot.

Nach und nach änderten sich die Dinge zum Besseren. Man sah Bläser auftreten, die mit Recht Künstler genannt werden konnten. Wie glänzend indessen auch diese Individualitäten waren, so konnten sie doch die Fehler ihres Ursprungs nicht verleugnen, d. h. den vollständigen Mangel an Vielseitigkeit und bestimmter Leitung. Bei diesen bewunderte man den höchsten Grad der Fertigkeit, jene wurden wegen des Ausdrucks ihres Spiels applaudirt. Die Einen wurden wegen ihrer Lippenkraft gerühmt, andere wegen der Leichtigkeit ihrer Höhe, andere endlich wegen des Glanzes oder Volumens ihres Tones. Es herrschte, um mich so auszudrücken, das Reich der Specialitäten. Aber man sieht nicht, dass ein einziger der beliebten Cornettisten jener Epoche daran gedacht oder es sich vorgesetzt hätte, die Summe dieser Qualitäten zu erlangen, welche allein den wahren Künstler ausmachen.

Dies ist der Punkt, bei welchem ich verweilen und auf den ich besonders die Aufmerksamkeit hinlenken wollte. In unserer Zeit hat man einstimmig die Unzulänglichkeit der alten Virtuosen sowie ihrer Art des Unterrichtes anerkannt. Was man verlangt ist methodische Ausbildung. Es genügt nicht, die Gesangstellen gut zu blasen oder die

AVANT-PROPOS.

Il peut paraître étrange ou superflu de venir prendre la défense du cornet à pistons, aujourd'hui que cet instrument a fait ses preuves dans l'orchestre et dans le solo; qu'il n'est pas moins indispensable au compositeur ni moins aimé du public que la flûte, la clarinette, et même le violon: aujourd'hui enfin qu'il a définitivement conquis le rang élevé que lui assignent la beauté de son timbre, la perfection de son mécanisme et l'immensité de ses ressources.

Mais il n'en a pas été toujours ainsi: le cornet a eu des commencements plus modestes, et il n'y a pas encore beaucoup d'années que les masses l'accueillaient avec une superbe indifférence, en même temps que le bataillon sacré de la routine contestait ses qualités, et s'efforçait d'en proscrire l'application, phénomène qui, d'ailleurs, ne manque jamais de se produire, à l'origine de toute invention nouvelle, si excellente soit-elle, et dont l'apparition du saxhorn et du saxophone, instruments plus jeunes que le cornet, a fourni une éclatante et nouvelle preuve.

Les premiers musiciens qui jouèrent du cornet à pistons furent en général des cornistes et des trompettistes. Chacun y apporta le cachet de ses goûts, de ses facultés, de ses habitudes, et je n'ai pas besoin d'ajouter qu'une exécution née d'éléments incomplets autant qu'hétérogènes, laissa bien longtemps à désirer, et offrit pendant une période assez prolongée le triste spectacle des lacunes, des défaillances et des défauts les plus choquants.

Peu à peu les choses se modifièrent dans un sens favorable; l'on vit surgir des exécutants véritablement dignes du nom d'artistes. Cependant, quelque brillantes que fussent ces individualités, elles ne purent se soustraire au vice de leur origine, c'est à-dire au manque absolu d'ensemble et de direction. Chez ceux-ci on admira une agilité extrême, ceux là se firent applaudir par l'expression de leur jeu; les uns furent cités pour leurs lèvres, les autres pour leur facilité à monter, d'autres enfin, pour l'éclat ou le volume de leur son: ce fut, si je puis parler ainsi, le règne de spécialités; mais on ne voit pas qu'un seul des cornettistes en vogue à cette époque, ait songé à réaliser ou se soit proposé d'acquérir la somme des qualités qui seules constituent les grands artistes.

C'est là le point sur lequel je voulais insister et particulièrement appeler l'attention. De nos jours, on a unanimement reconnu l'insuffisance des anciens virtuoses, comme aussi l'insuffisance de leur enseignement. Ce que l'on veut, c'est une exécution, c'est un enseignement méthodique; il ne suffit pas de bien chanter ou de bien faire la difficulté, il faut faire égale

In a word, it is necessary that the cornet, as well as the flute, the clarinet, the violin, and the voice, should possess the pure style and the grand method of which a few professors, the Conservatory in particular, have conserved the precious secret and the salutary traditions.

This is the aim which I have incessantly kept in view throughout my long career; and if a numerous series of brilliant successes (obtained in the presence of the most competent judges and the most critical audiences),* give me the right to believe that I have, at any rate, approached the desired end, I shall not be laying myself open to the charge of presumption, in confidently entering upon the delicate mission of transmitting to others the results of my own thorough studies and assiduous practice. I have long been a professor, and this work is to a certain extent, merely the resumé of a long experience, which each day has brought nearer to perfection.

My explanations will be found as short and clear as possible, for I wish to instruct and not to terrify the student. Long pages of "text" are not always read, and it is highly advantageous to replace the latter by exercises and examples. This is the wealth which I consider cannot be too lavishly accumulated; this is the source which can never be too plentifully drawn from. This, however, will be perceived from the extent of the present volume, in which, in my opinion, will be found the solution of all difficulties and of all problems.

I have endeavored throughout to compose studies of a melodic nature, and in general to render the study of the instrument as agreeable as possible. In a word, I have endeavored to lead the pupil, without discouragement, to the highest limits of execution, sentiment and style, destined to characterize the new school.

J. B. ARBAN.

---

*) The results which I have obtained in France, Germany and England victoriously plead the cause of the cornet and prove that the latter can compete with the most popular of instruments. In a concert given by the "Societé des Concerts du Conservatoire" in 1848, I played the famous air for the flute composed by Boehm on a Swiss theme, comprising, as is well known, an intentional combination of enormous difficulties. From that day forth I may say the cornet took its place among classic instruments. In the piece of music just alluded to, I performed the flute tonguing in double staccato, also the triple staccato, which I am the first to have applied to the cornet.

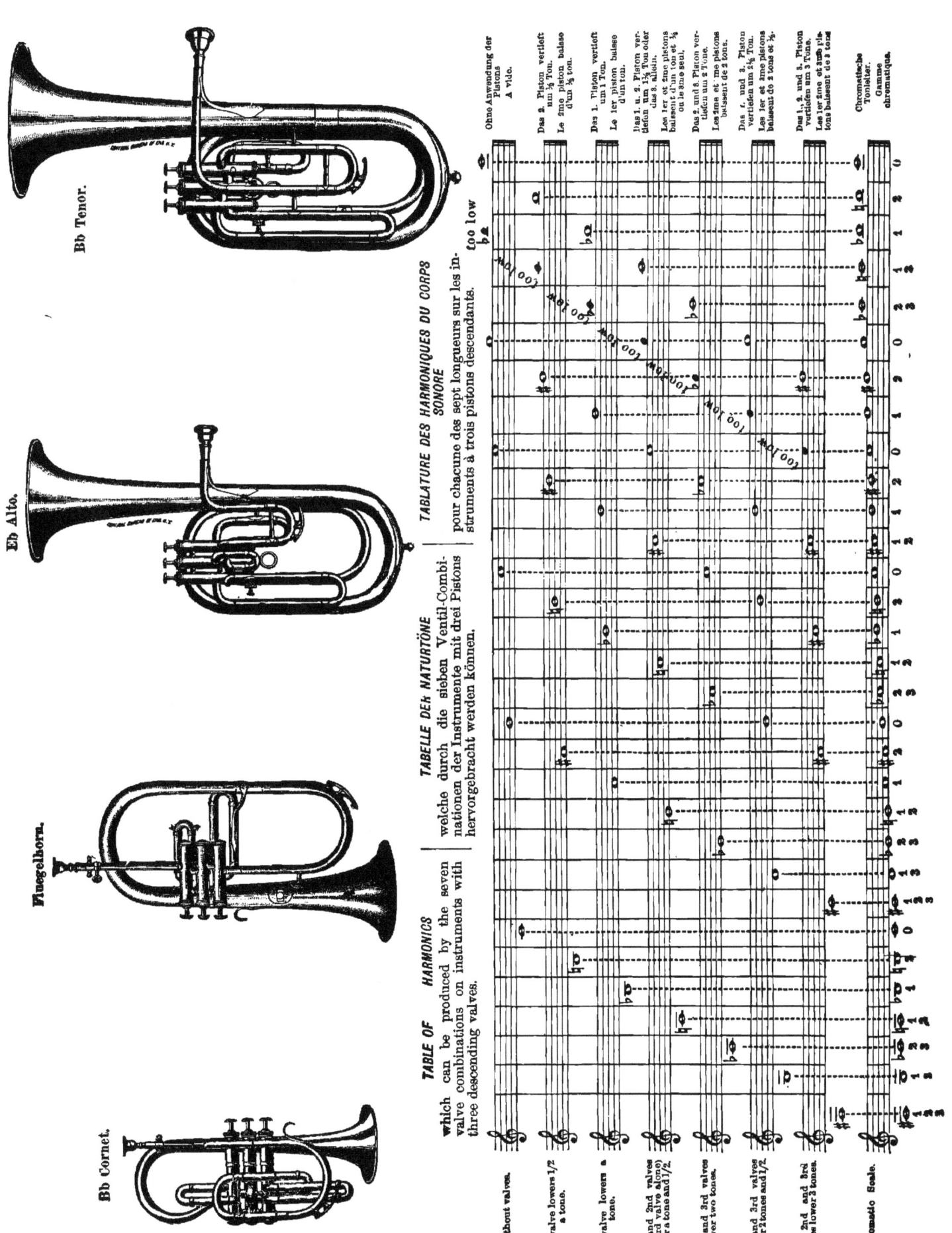

DIAGRAM OF CORNET
Giving Proper Names to the Various Parts of the Instrument

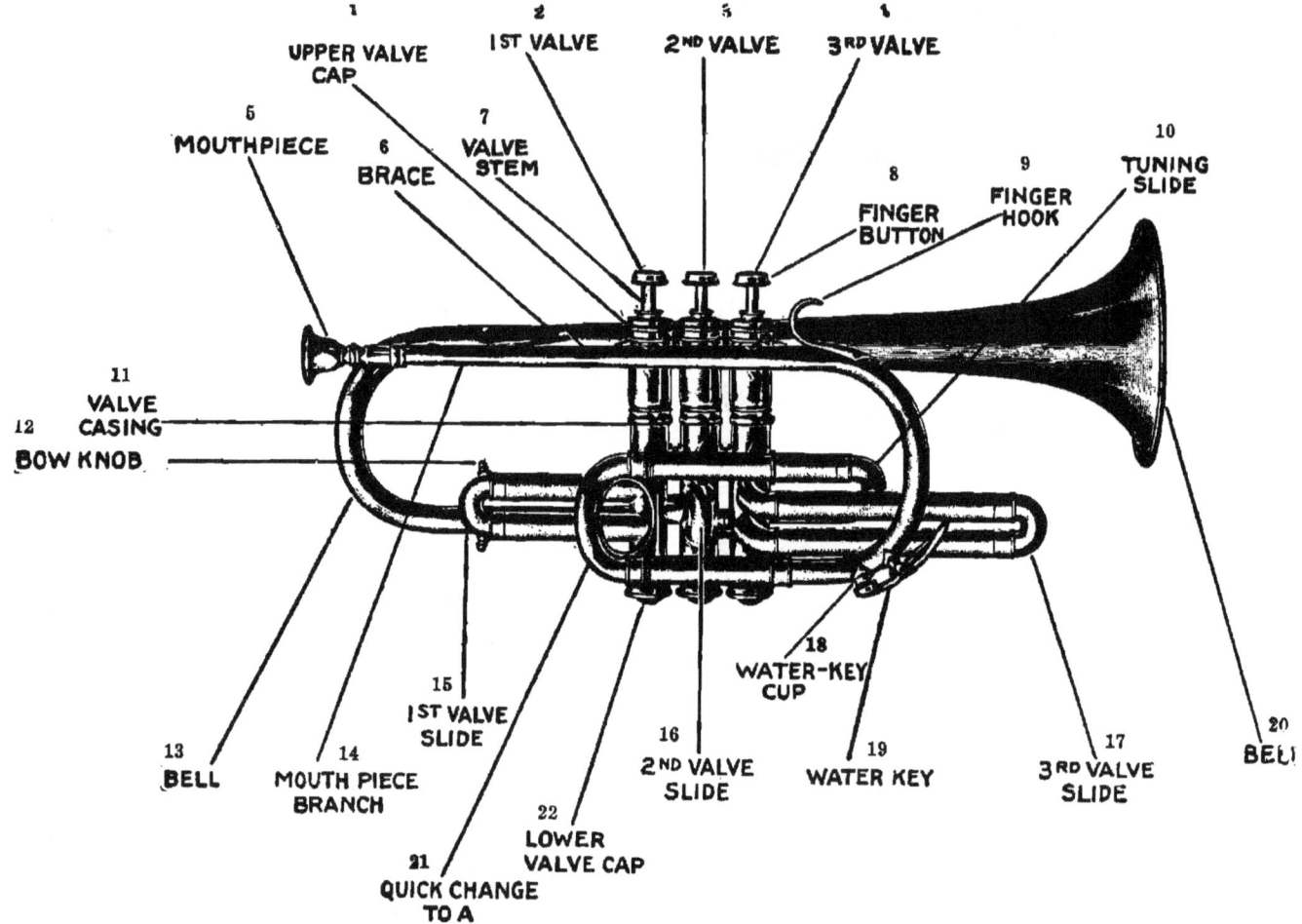

The Cornet pictured above is a Besson New Creation (Long Model)

ABBILDUNG EINES CORNETS
Mit richtiger Bezeichnung der verschiedenen Teile des Instruments

1. Oberer Ventilschraubendeckel
2. 1-stes Ventil
3. 2-tes Ventil
4. 3-tes Ventil
5. Mundstück
6. Stütze
7. Ventilstange
8. Fingerknopf
9. Fingerhaken
10. Stimmzug
11. Aeusere Ventilhülse
12. Bogenknöpfchen
13. Schallbecherbogen
14. Mundstückröhre
15. 1-ster Ventilzug
16. 2-ter Ventilzug
17. 3-ter Ventilzug
18. Wasserklappenhülse
19. Wasserklappe
20. Schallbecher
21. Schnell-Wechsel Bogen für A Stimmung
22. Unterer Ventilschraubendeckel

DAS OBEN ABGEBILDETE CORNET IST EIN BESSON NEUER STYL (Langes Model)

ILLUSTRATION D'UM CORNET
Avec propre appelation des diverse parties du cornet

1. Chapeau du piston
2. 1-er piston
3. 2-me piston
4. 3-me piston
5. Embouchure du Cornet à piston
6. Traverse pour Soliditèr
7. Branche du piston
8. Boutons des pistons
9. Support du Cornet pour le petit doigt
10. Coulisse d'accord
11. Le tube des pistons ou Magasin
12. Support de la Coulisse
13. Grand tube ou pavillon
14. Coulisse de l'embouchure
15. 1-er coulisse
16. 2-me coulisse
17. 3-me coulisse
18. Bassin de la clef d'eau
19. Clef d'eau
20. Pavillon
21. Transpositeur de Sib en la
22. Cuvettes des pistons

LE CORNET ICI ILLUSTRÉ EST UN BESSON NOUVEAU STYL (MODEL ELONGÉ)

Compass of the Cornet.

As indicated in the accompanying table, the instruments with three valves have a chromatic range of two octaves and a half, which, in the case of the cornet and the alto, extends from F sharp below to C above the staff; however, not every player succeeds in mastering the whole of this range with clearness and facility. Therefore, when writing for these instruments, even if it is for a solo, it will be advisable not to use the extreme limits of the scale indicated in the foregoing table. As a rule, the higher registers of the instruments are employed much too frequently by arrangers and composers, in consequence of which the performer is apt to lose the beautiful and characteristic tonal qualities peculiar to his instrument. It also leads to failure to produce the simplest passages, even when called for in the middle register. To avoid this evil, it is necessary to continually practice the instrument throughout its entire register, and to pay special attention to the chapter devoted to the study of the various intervals.

The easiest portion of the cornet's range commences at low C and terminates at G above the staff. One may easily ascend as high as B flat, but the B natural and the C ought to be made use of very sparingly.

In regard to the notes below C:

same do not present any very great difficulties, although some players experience considerable trouble in producing them with clearness and sonority. However, when properly produced, they are very beautiful and effective.

Cornet in C

It is indispensably necessary that the performer should play the cornets in C and B natural, as well as the one in B flat, as they may prove of great service in orchestra, especially for the performance of trumpet parts.

The cornet in C is a most brilliant solo instrument, its timbre, in some respects, being more preferable than that of the cornet in B flat. In theatres devoted to the performance of lyric works it is really indispensable on account of the ease and surety with which the highest intervals can be produced, and also on account of transpositions which are much easier on this than on the B flat cornet. If an orchestra number is written in the key of B natural, or in E major, it is advisable to play on a cornet pitched in B natural. If written in C or F the cornet in C should be employed. As for the cornet in A, it accords but poorly with any of the keys I have just been indicating, and its use would only serve to create unnecessary difficulties.*

---

*) Since the above was written, the cornet, together with every other wind instrument, has been brought to such a high state of perfection, as to do away entirely with many of the drawbacks of the old system. Nowadays the cornet in C is used to some slight extent by amateurs who desire to play from vocal music and who through use of this instrument avoid the necessity of transposition. It is seldom used by professionals. The cornet in B natural is entirely obsolete. —*The Editor.*

Second Table.

Suggestions are offered herewith for producing F natural below the staff and at the same time for facilitating certain passages, which, with the fingering indicated in the first table, are well-nigh impossible. In order to achieve this, the slide of the third valve should be drawn out one-half tone, in order to obtain a length of two tones, instead of the usual one and one-half tones. In doing this, it will be advisable to adopt the following fingering, which is very popular among German Cavalry trumpeters.

Zweite Tabelle.

Es giebt ein Mittel, das *F* unter den Linien zu erhalten, und zugleich die Ausführung gewisser Passagen zu erleichtern, welche mit dem in der ersten Tabelle angegebenen Fingersatze unausführbar sind. Zu diesem Zwecke muss man den Zugbogen des dritten Pistons um einen halben Ton herausziehen, um so eine Länge von zwei Tönen zu erhalten anstatt der gewöhnlichen von 1½ Ton. Man wird sich dann des folgenden Fingersatzes bedienen, der übrigens in Deutschland bei Cavallerie-Musik sehr gebräuchlich ist.

Deuxième Tablature.

Il existe un moyen d'obtenir le *fa* naturel au-dessous des lignes, et en même temps de faciliter l'exécution de certains passages impraticables avec les doigtés indiqués sur la première tablature. Il faut, pour cela, tirer d'un demi-ton la coulisse du troisième piston, de manière à réaliser une longueur de deux tons, au lieu d'un ton et demi qu'elle possède habituellement. On se servira alors du doigté suivant qui, d'ailleurs, est fort usité en Allemagne.

In order that the F natural may be produced in perfect tune, the tuning slide should be drawn out a little. (I shall explain this more fully in the next chapter.)
Example of trills impossible with the ordinary fingering, but quite easy with the fingering as shown in this second table.

Man muss, damit das *F* vollständig rein wird, zu gleicher Zeit den Stimmbogen ein wenig herausziehen, wie ich in dem nächsten Capitel mittheilen werde.
Beispiel der mit dem gewöhnlichen Fingersatz unausführbaren Triller, die man aber leicht bei Anwendung des Fingersatzes der zweiten Tabelle hervorbringen kann:

Il faut, pour que le *fa* naturel soit tout à fait juste, tirer en même temps un peu la coulisse d'accord, ainsi que je l'indiquerai dans le prochain chapitre.
Exemple de trilles impraticables avec le doigté ordinaire, et que l'on peut obtenir facilement en employant le doigté de la deuxième tablature:

Examples of special passages, showing how forked fingering may be avoided:

Beispiel einiger Figuren, in welchen man bei Anwendung desselben Fingersatzes die Gabeln vermeiden kann:

Exemples de quelques traits dans lesquels on peut éviter les fourches en employant ce même doigté:

Only in exceptional cases should expedients such as the above be employed. I have only called attention to them here in order to acquaint the student with all the resources of the instrument.

Man darf nur in Ausnahmefällen zu diesem Verfahren seine Zuflucht nehmen; ich gebe es hier nur, um mit allen Hülfsmitteln des Instrumentes bekannt zu machen.

On ne doit recourir à ces procédés que dans des cas exceptionnels; je ne les donne ici que pour faire bien connaître toutes les ressources de l'instrument.

Use of the Tuning Slide

A well-constructed cornet ought to be so mounted that the thumb of the left hand should be able to enter the ring of the tuning slide, and open and shut it at pleasure, without the help of the right hand. It is then possible to regulate the pitch of the instrument while playing. It is generally known that when beginning to play with a cold instrument the latter will always be a little below pitch. After a few measures have been played, and the instrument is warmed, it will sharpen very rapidly.

The slide is also used for the purpose of equalizing all those notes which, in the course of natural production, are rendered too high. Each valve is tuned for separate use, and the natural consequence is that when several are employed simultaneously the slides get too short and the precision of tone is inevitably affected. Here is a practical example: Let us suppose that the player will use a G crook on a B flat cornet; this will lower the instrument one tone and a half. In order to play in tune in this new key it will be necessary to draw out the slide of each valve considerably.

*) In the estimation of acknowledged modern authorities on cornet playing, there is no necessity for playing the F below the staff, as it is really not within the legitimate range of the instrument.—*The Editor.*

Anwendung des Stimmbogens.

Ein gut gearbeitetes Cornet à pistons soll so beschaffen sein, dass der Daumen der linken Hand in den Ring des Stimmbogens hineingehen kann, um ihn ohne Hülfe der rechten Hand nach Belieben zu öffnen und zu schliessen. Man kann also während des Blasens stimmen. Jedermann weiss, dass wenn man anfängt zu spielen, das Instrument, da es kalt ist, ein wenig zu tief steht. Erst nach der Ausführung einiger Takte steigt das Instrument, indem es warm wird, und zwar in einem ausserordentlichen Verhältniss.

Der Stimmbogen soll dazu dienen, die Töne, welche von Natur zu hoch sind, auszugleichen. Da jedes Piston abgestimmt ist, um es einzeln anzuwenden, so werden, wenn man mehrere zusammenfügt, die Zugbogen zu kurz und die Genauigkeit leidet darunter. Hier ein Beispiel: Gesetzt, man brächte auf das Cornet à pistons in *B* ein Versatzstück, und dieses wäre der Ton *G*, so steht das Instrument 1½ Ton tiefer. Um in der neuen Stimmung richtig zu blasen ist es nothwendig, den Bogen eines jeden Pistons bedeutend auszuziehen.

Emploi de la coulisse d'accord.

Un cornet à pistons bien fabriqué doit être monté de manière à ce que le pouce de la main gauche puisse entrer dans l'anneau de la coulisse d'accord, afin de pouvoir l'ouvrir et la fermer à volonté sans le secours de la main droite. On peut ainsi s'accorder en jouant; personne n'ignore que lorsqu'on commence à jouer, l'instrument, étant froid, se trouve un peu trop bas. Ce n'est qu'après l'exécution de quelques mesures que l'instrument monte en s'échauffant, et cela dans des proportions extraordinaires.

La coulisse d'accord doit servir aussi à compenser les notes qui, par leur nature, sont trop hautes. Chaque piston étant accordé pour être employé séparément, quand on en additionne plusieurs, les coulisses deviennent forcément trop courtes, et la justesse se trouve altérée. En voici un exemple: Supposez que sur le cornet à pistons en *si* bémol vous mettiez un corps de rechange, et que ce soit le ton de *sol*, l'instrument se trouve alors baissé d'un ton et demi. Pour jouer juste avec ce nouveau ton, il faut nécessairement tirer beaucoup la coulisse de chaque piston.

A similar effect is produced whenever the third valve is employed. For instance, when the third valve is pressed down on a B flat cornet, the latter is lowered one tone and a half; the effect is exactly as though the instrument were pitched in G, as the slides of each valve produce the effect of tones added to the instrument.

In such a case it would be necessary to draw the slides of the first and second valves in order to use them simultaneously with the third. But as such a proceeding is most impractical, it will be advisable to employ the above-mentioned device; that is, compensate for the want of length of the tubes by drawing the slide with the thumb of the left hand. Without this precaution every one of the following notes would be too high.

Eine gleiche Wirkung zeigt sich allemal, wenn man auf irgend einem Instrument das dritte Piston in Anwendung bringt. Wenn man auf dem *B*-Cornet das dritte Piston tiefer stellt, so macht man dasselbe um 1½ Ton tiefer; das ist gerade so, als ob man ein Instrument in *G* hat, da die Zugbogen eines jeden Pistons die Wirkung der Töne hervorbringen, welche dem Instrument durch Versatzstücke hinzugefügt sind.

In diesem Falle würde man die Bogen des ersten und zweiten Pistons herausziehen müssen, um sich ihrer in Gemeinschaft mit dem dritten bedienen zu können. Da aber diese Operation nicht gut thunlich ist, so wird es nothwendig, sich durch das oben angeführte Kunststück zu helfen, das heisst, was den Röhren an Länge gebricht, dadurch auszugleichen, dass man mit dem Daumen der linken Hand den Stimmbogen herauszieht; ohne diese Vorsichtsmaassregel würden alle Töne zu hoch werden.

Un effet analogue se produit toutes les fois que sur un instrument quelconque vous employez le troisième piston. Ainsi, lorsque sur un cornet en *si* bémol vous abaissez le troisième piston, vous le baissez d'un ton et demi: c'est exactement comme si vous aviez mis votre instrument en *sol*, puisque les coulisses de chaque piston produisent l'effet de tons ajoutés à l'instrument.

Il faudrait donc, dans ce cas, tirer les coulisses du premier et du deuxième piston, pour s'en servir collectivement avec le troisième, mais comme cette opération est impracticable, il devient nécessaire d'y suppléer l'artifice indiqué ci-dessous, c'est-à dire de compenser le manque de longueur des tubes, en tirant la coulisse d'accord avec le pouce de la main gauche; sans cette précaution, toutes les notes ci-après seraient trop hautes.

It is not difficult to lower these notes through action of the lips, although the quality of the tone will invariably suffer through such a proceeding. Therefore, in order to insure proper tonal brilliancy, it is always better in slow movements to employ the slide as a compensatory medium.

Es ist nicht schwer, diese Töne vermittelst der Lippen herabzustimmen, aber dies geschieht auf Kosten der Güte des Tons. Es ist also besser in langsamen Tempo's, um dem Tone seinen vollen Glanz zu bewahren, sich des Stimmbogens zur Ausgleichung zu bedienen.

Il n'est pas difficile de descendre ces notes au moyen des lèvres, mais c'est au prix de la qualité du son. Il vaut donc mieux, dans les mouvements lents, pour conserver au son tout son éclat, se servir de la coulisse d'accord comme compensateur.

Position of the Mouthpiece on the Lips.

The mouthpiece should be placed in the middle of the lips, two-thirds on the lower lip, and one-third on the upper lip. At any rate, this is the position which I myself have adopted, and which I believe to be the best.

Horn players generally place the mouthpiece two-thirds on the upper lip and one-third on the lower, which is precisely the reverse of what I have just recommended for the cornet; but it must not be forgotten that great difference exists in the formation of this instrument as well as in the method of holding it, and that which may admirably suit the horn, is attended with very bad results when applied to the cornet. What, after all, is the principal object as regards the position of the cornet? Why, that it should be perfectly horizontal. Well, then, if the mouthpiece were placed as though the performer were playing the horn, the instrument would be in a falling position, resembling that of the clarinet.

Some teachers make a point of changing the position of the mouthpiece previously adopted by the pupils who apply to them. I have seldom known this method to succeed. To my own knowledge, several players, already possessed of remarkable talent, have attempted what we call at the Conservatoire, the "orthopedic system," which consists in rectifying and correcting the wrong placing of the mouthpiece. I consider it my duty to say that these artists, after having wasted several years in uselessly trying the system in question, were compelled to return to their primitive mode of placing the mouthpiece, not one of them having obtained any advantage, while some of them were no longer able to play at all.

Stellung des Mundstücks auf den Lippen.

Das Mundstück soll in der Mitte des Mundes stehen, zwei Drittel auf der Unterlippe, und ein Drittel auf der Oberlippe; das ist wenigstens die Stellung, die ich für mich selbst angenommen habe, und die ich für die beste halte.

Die Hornisten setzen in der Regel zwei Drittel auf die Oberlippe und ein Drittel auf die Unterlippe, was gerade das Gegentheil wäre von dem, was ich so eben vom Cornet gesagt habe; man muss aber nicht vergessen, dass es in der Bauart des Instruments, wie in der Art, es zu halten, grosse Verschiedenheiten giebt, und was dem Horne sehr wohl zusagen kann, ist bei dem Cornet à pistons von einer schlechten Wirkung. Was soll man also von der Haltung des Cornet à pistons wünschen? dass sie horizontal sei. Wenn man nun das Mundstück so stellt, wie man es beim Horne gewöhnt ist, so erhält das Instrument die Richtung des Falles, als ob man Clarinette bliese.

Es giebt Lehrer, welche die Gewohnheit haben, den Ansatz des Mundstückes bei allen Schülern, die sich an sie wenden, zu verändern. Ich habe selten dieses System mit Erfolg angewandt gesehen. Mehrere Künstler meiner Bekanntschaft, die schon ein beachtungswerthes Talent besassen, haben versucht, was wir am Conservatorium "*le système orthopédique*" nennen, welches darin besteht, den schlechten Ansatz des Mundstücks zu verbessern. Ich muss sagen, dass diese Künstler, nachdem sie mehrere Jahre unnützer Arbeit nach diesem Systeme verloren hatten, gezwungen waren, ihr Mundstück wieder wie früher anzusetzen, denn Niemand hatte ein gutes Resultat erhalten, Einige sogar konnten gar nicht mehr blasen.

Position de l'embouchure sur les lèvres.

L'embouchure doit se poser au milieu de la bouche, deux tiers sur la lèvre inférieure et un tiers sur la lèvre supérieure, c'est du moins la position que j'ai adoptée pour moi-même, et que je crois la meilleure.

Les cornistes posent généralement l'embouchure deux tiers sur la lèvre supérieure et un tiers sur la lèvre inférieure, ce qui est justement le contraire de ce que je viens d'indiquer pour le cornet; mais il ne faut pas oublier qu'il y a de grandes différences dans la conformation de l'instrument comme dans la manière de le tenir; et ce qui peut très-bien convenir au cor est d'un mauvais effet avec le cornet. Ainsi, que doit-on désirer dans la position du cornet à pistons? qu'il soit bien horizontal; eh bien, si on plaçait l'embouchure comme on a coutume de le faire pour le cor, l'instrument aurait une tendance à tomber, comme si on jouait de la clarinette.

Il y a des professeurs qui ont pour habitude de changer la position d'embouchure de tous les élèves qui s'adressent à eux. J'ai rarement vu ce système réussir; à ma connaissance, plusieurs artistes, possédant déjà un talent remarquable, ont essayé de ce que nous appelons au Conservatoire le système orthopédique, lequel consiste à redresser les embouchures mal placées. Je dois dire que ces mêmes artistes, après avoir perdu plusieurs années à travailler inutilement d'après ce système, furent obligés d'en revenir à placer leur embouchure dans la position primitive, car aucun n'avait obtenu de bons résultats, quelques-uns même ne pouvaient plus jouer du tout.

From all this I conclude that when a player has commenced his studies faultily, he must, of course, endeavor to improve himself, but must not change the position of his mouthpiece, especially if he has already attained a certain degree of proficiency, it being a known fact that there is no lack of performers who play perfectly, and who even possess a most beautiful tone, and who, nevertheless, place their mouthpiece at the side, and even at the corners of the mouth. All that can be done is to beware of acquiring this faulty habit. In short, there is no absolute rule for the position of the mouthpiece, for everything depends upon the formation of the mouth and the regularity of the teeth.

The mouthpiece, once placed, must not be moved either for ascending or descending passages. It would be impossible to execute certain passages if the performer were compelled to change the position of the mouthpiece whenever he wished to take a low note after a high one in rapid succession.

In order to produce the higher notes, it is necessary to press the instrument against the lips, so as to produce an amount of tension proportionate to the needs of the note to be produced; the lips being thus stretched, the vibrations are shorter, and the sounds are consequently of a higher nature.

For descending passages it is necessary to apply the mouthpiece more lightly, in order to allow a larger opening for the passage of air. The vibrations then become slower owing to the relaxation of the muscles, and lower sounds are thus obtained in proportion to the extent to which the lips are opened.

The lips must never be protruded. On the contrary, the corners of the mouth must be drawn down, enabling a freer, more open tone production. When the lips begin to tire the performer should never force his tones. He should then play more piano, because with continued loud playing the lips swell, and at last it becomes impossible to emit a note. The performer should cease to play the moment the lips begin to feel weak and fatigued; in fact, it is folly to continue playing under such circumstances, as it might lead to an affection of the lip which might take a long time to cure.

Method of Striking or Commencing the Tone.

It should never be lost sight of, that the expression *coup de langue* (stroke of the tongue) is merely a conventional expression; the tongue does not strike; on the contrary, it performs a retrograde movement; it simply supplies the place of a valve.

This circumstance should be well borne in mind before placing the mouthpiece on the lips. The tongue ought to be placed against the teeth of the upper jaw in such a way that the mouth should be hermetically sealed. As the tongue recedes, the column of air which was pressing against it is precipitated violently into the mouthpiece and causes the sound.

Ich habe daraus den Schluss gezogen, dass, wenn ein Künstler einmal schlecht angefangen hat, er nur bestrebt sein soll, sich zu vervollkommnen, nicht aber seinen Ansatz zu wechseln, besonders wenn er bereits eine gewisse Geschicklichkeit erreicht hat, denn es fehlt nicht an Virtuosen, die vortrefflich blasen und einen sehr schönen Ton haben, und doch ihr Mundstück auf die Seite, ja sogar in den Winkel des Mundes setzen. Alles, was man thun kann, ist, sich vor diesem Fehler zu hüten. Alles in Allem, um mich kurz zu fassen: Es giebt keine absolute Regel für den Ansatz des Mundstücks, denn Alles hängt von der Bildung des Mundes, wie von der Regelmässigkeit der Zähne ab.

Ist das Mundstück einmal angesetzt, so darf es nicht verschoben werden, weder bei höheren noch bei tieferen Tönen. Man muss diese Resultate durch die Biegsamkeit der Lippen erzielen. Es wäre unmöglich, gewisse Passagen auszuführen, wenn man gezwungen wäre, bei einem schnellen Uebergange von einem hohen nach einem tiefen Tone den Ansatz zu wechseln.

Um die hohen Töne hervorzubringen, ist es erforderlich, einen gewissen Druck auf die Lippen auszuüben, und zwar der Art, um ihnen eine Spannung zu verleihen, die im Verhältniss zu der Höhe der Note steht, welche man zu erhalten wünscht; sind die Lippen in dieser Weise gespannt, so werden die Vibrationen kürzer, und folgerecht die Töne höher.

Um abwärts zu gehen muss man im Gegentheil das Mundstück leichter ansetzen, um dem Durchzuge der Luft mehr Raum zu gewähren. In Folge der Abspannung der Muskeln werden die Vibrationen dann langsamer, und man erhält die tiefen Töne, conform mit dem Grade der Oeffnung, welche man den Lippen lässt.

Man muss niemals die Lippen nach vorwärts führen; im Gegentheil muss man die Mundwinkel ziehen; durch dieses Mittel erhält man einen viel offeneren Ton. Wenn die Lippen zu erschlaffen anfangen, muss man niemals die Töne forciren; man muss dann mehr piano blasen; denn bei starkem Blasen schwellen die Lippen, und es wird unmöglich einen Ton hervorzubringen. Man muss zu blasen aufhören, sobald die Muskeln anfangen zu erlahmen. Es würde eine Thorheit sein, dann noch fortzufahren, da dies leicht eine Steifheit der Lippen zur Folge haben könnte, welche längere Zeit anhält.

Ueber die Art, den Ton anzusetzen.

Man darf nicht aus dem Auge verlieren, dass der Ausdruck: "Zungenstoss" nur ein conventionelles Wort ist. In Wirklichkeit giebt die Zunge keinen Stoss; im Gegentheil, anstatt zu stossen, macht sie eine Bewegung nach rückwärts; sie erfüllt einzig und allein den Dienst eines Ventils.

Man muss sich von dieser Wirkung Rechenschaft ablegen, bevor man das Mundstück an die Lippen setzt. Die Zunge soll gegen die Zähne des Oberkiefers gedrückt werden, der Art, dass der Mund hermetisch geschlossen ist. In dem Augenblicke, in welchem sich die Zunge zurückzieht, stürzt sich die Luftsäule, welche den Druck auf sie ausübt, heftig in das Mundstück und bringt den Ton hervor.

Je conclus de ceci que, lorsqu'un artiste a mal commencé, il doit seulement chercher à se perfectionner, mais non à changer son embouchure de place, surtout s'il est déjà d'une certaine force, attendu qu'il ne manque pas de virtuoses qui jouent parfaitement et qui ont même un très-beau son, tout en posant leur embouchure sur le côté et même dans les coins de la bouche. Tout ce que l'on peut faire, c'est de se mettre en garde contre ce défaut. En somme, et pour me résumer, il n'y a aucune règle absolue pour la pose de l'embouchure, car tout dépend de la conformation de la bouche et de la régularité des dents.

L'embouchure une fois posée, il ne faut plus la déranger ni pour monter, ni pour descendre; on doit obtenir ces résultats par la flexibilité des lèvres. Il serait impossible d'exécuter de certains passages, si on était obligé de changer l'embouchure de place pour prendre avec rapidité une note grave après une note élevée.

Pour faire sortir les notes hautes, il est nécessaire d'opérer une certaine pression sur les lèvres, de manière à leur donner une tension proportionnée au degré de la note qu'on veut obtenir: les lèvres étant ainsi tendues, les vibrations deviennent plus courtes, et par conséquent les sons plus élevés.

Pour descendre, il faut, au contraire, appuyer l'embouchure plus légèrement, afin de donner plus d'ouverture au passage de l'air: les vibrations étant alors plus lentes par l'effet du relâchement des muscles, on obtient des sons graves conformes au degré d'ouverture que l'on donne aux lèvres.

Il ne faut jamais ramener les lèvres en avant; il faut, au contraire, tirer les coins de la bouche: par ce moyen, on obtient un son beaucoup plus ouvert. Lorsque les lèvres commencent à être fatiguées, il ne faut jamais forcer les sons; jouez alors plus piano; car, en jouant fort, les lèvres se gonflent, et il devient impossible de faire sortir une note. On doit cesser de jouer quand les muscles commencent à se paralyser; il y aurait folie à continuer, attendu qu'il s'ensuivrait peut-être des courbatures de lèvres qui pourraient durer fort long-temps.

Manière d'attaquer le son.

Il ne faut pas perdre de vue que l'expression. coup de langue n'est qu'un mot de convention; la langue, en effet, ne donne pas de coup: car, au lieu de frapper, elle opère, au contraire, un mouvement en arrière; elle remplit seulement l'office d'une soupape.

Il faut se rendre bien compte de cet effet, avant de poser l'embouchure sur les lèvres. La langue doit être placée contre les dents de la mâchoire supérieure, de manière à ce que la bouche soit hermétiquement fermée. Au moment où la langue se retire, la colonne d'air qui fait pression sur elle, se précipite violemment dans l'embouchure et produit le son.

The pronunciation of the syllable "Tu" serves to determine the striking of the sound. This syllable may be pronounced with more or less softness, according to the degree of force to be imparted to the note. When a long dash is placed over a note

Die Aussprache der Sylbe *tü* dient dazu den Tonansatz bestimmt zu machen. Diese Sylbe kann mehr oder weniger sanft ausgesprochen werden, je nach dem Grade der Stärke, den man mit dem Ansatz hervorbringen will. Sobald über einer Note ein verlängerter Punkt steht,

La prononciation de la syllabe *tu* sert à déterminer l'attaque du son. Cette syllabe peut être prononcée avec plus ou moins de douceur, suivant le degré de force que vous voulez donner à votre attaque. Lorsque sur une note il y a un point allongé

it indicates that the sound ought to be very short; the syllable ought then to be uttered very briefly and dryly. When, on the contrary, there is only a dot,

so bezeichnet dies, dass der Ton sehr kurz sein soll; die Sylbe *tü* muss dann sehr kurz ausgesprochen werden. Wenn aber als Gegensatz nur ein Punkt über einer Note steht,

cela indique que le son doit être fort court vous devez alors prononcer la syllabe *tu* avec beaucoup de sécheresse. Lorsque, au contraire il n'y a qu'un point

the syllable should be pronounced with more softness, so that the sounds, although detached, still form a connected phrase. When, upon a succession of notes, there are dots over which there is a slur,

so muss die Sylbe mit mehr Weichheit ausgesprochen werden, der Art, dass die Töne, obgleich gestosen, sich dennoch unter einander verbinden. Wenn man bei einer Folge von Noten über die Punkte noch eine Bindung setzt,

vous devez prononcer cette syllabe avec plus de douceur, de manière que les sons, quoique détachés, se lient bien entre eux. Quand, sur une succession de notes, on met des points au dessus desquels il y a un coulé

the performer should invariably strike the note with a very soft "Tu," and then substitute for it the syllable "Du," because the latter syllable not only distinctly articulates each note, but also serves admirably to join notes together.

These are the only three methods of commencing, or, as it is called, "striking," the sound. Further on I will duly explain the various articulations. For the present, it is only necessary to know and to practice the simple tonguing, for upon this starting point the pupil's future excellence as an executant depends entirely.

As I have already said, the method of "striking" the sound immediately shows whether the performer possesses a good or faulty style. The first part of this method is entirely devoted to studies of this description, and I shall not pass on to the slur until the pupil has thoroughly mastered the striking of the note.

so muss man die erste Note mit einem sehr sanften *tü* angeben, und dieses *tü* dann durch *dü* substituiren, da diese Sylbe, indem man jede Note ausspricht, dieselben unter einander bindet. (Man nennt dies den Zungenstoss im Tone.)

Es giebt nur diese drei Arten, die Töne anzusetzen, d. h. sie zu trennen. Später werde ich die anderen Articulationen zur Kenntniss bringen. Für jetzt ist es nur am Ort, den einfachen Zungenstoss zu kennen und zu studiren, denn von diesem Ausgangspunkte hängt lediglich der Erfolg einer guten Ausführung ab.

Wie ich bereits oben gesagt habe, lässt die Art des Tonansatzes unverzüglich erkennen, ob Jemand einen guten oder schlechten Styl hat. Der erste Theil dieser Schule ist gänzlich dieser Gattung von Etuden gewidmet: ich werde erst zu den Bindungen übergehen, wenn der Schüler den Tonansatz vollständig inne hat.

vous devez invariablement poser la première note avec un *tu* très-doux, et lui substituer ensuite la syllabe *du*, par la raison que cette syllabe, tout en articulant chaque note, les lie parfaitement entre elles. (C'est ce que l'on nomme le coup de langue dans le son.)

Il n'y a que ces trois manières d'attaquer, c'est-à-dire de séparer les sons; plus tard, je ferai connaître les autres articulations. Pour le moment, il n'y a lieu de connaître et d'étudier que le coup de langue simple, car de ce point de départ dépend entièrement le succès d'une bonne exécution.

Comme je l'ai dit plus haut, la manière d'attaquer le son laisse voir immédiatement si vous avez un bon ou un mauvais style. La première partie de cette méthode est entièrement consacrée à ce genre d'études; je ne passerai aux coulés que quand l'élève saura parfaitement attaquer et poser le son.

Method of Breathing.

The mouthpiece having been placed on the lips, the mouth should partly open at the sides, and the tongue retire, in order to allow the air to penetrate into the lungs. The stomach ought not to swell, but, on the contrary, rather recede, in proportion as the chest is dilated by the respiration.

The tongue should then advance against the teeth of the upper jaw in such a way as to hermetically close the mouth, as though it were a valve intended to keep the column of air in the lungs.

The instant the tongue recedes, the air which has been pressing against it precipitates itself into the instrument and determines the vibrations which produce the sound. The stomach should then gradually resume its primitive position in proportion as the chest is lightened by the diminution of the air in the lungs.

Ueber die Art zu athmen.

Ist das Mundstück einmal auf die Lippen gesetzt, so soll sich der Mund nach den Seiten hin öffnen, und die Zunge sich zurückziehen, um die Luft in die Lungen einzulassen. Der Bauch soll sich nicht blähen, sondern soll im Gegentheil zurücktreten, je nachdem die Brust durch das Einathmen aufschwillt.

Die Zunge soll dann gegen die obere Zahnreihe vorgehen, der Art, dass der Mund hermetisch geschlossen wird, wie eine Klappe es bewirken würde, welche da ist, um die Luftsäule in den Lungen zu erhalten.

In dem Augenblicke, wo die Zunge sich zurückzieht, stürzt die Luft, welche den Druck auf sie ausübte, in das Instrument und bestimmt die Schwingungen, welche den Ton hervorbringen. Der Bauch soll dann langsam seine frühere Stellung wieder einnehmen, der Abnahme folgend, welche die Brust durch die Verminderung der Luft in den Lungen bewirkt.

Manière de respirer.

L'embouchure une fois placée sur les lèvres, la bouche doit s'entr'ouvrir sur les côtés, et la langue se retirer pour laisser pénétrer l'air dans les poumons. Le ventre ne doit pas se gonfler, il doit, au contraire, remonter au fur et à mesure que la poitrine grossit par l'effet de l'aspiration.

La langue doit alors s'avancer contre les dents de la mâchoire supérieure, de manière à fermer hermétiquement la bouche, comme le ferait une soupape chargée de maintenir la colonne d'air dans les poumons.

Au moment où la langue se retire, l'air qui faisait pression sur elle se précipite dans l'instrument et détermine les vibrations qui produisent le son. Le ventre alors doit reprendre doucement sa position primitive, en suivant le décroissement que la poitrine opère par l'effet de la diminution de l'air dans les poumons.

The breathing ought to be regulated by the length of the passage to be executed. In short phrases, if the breath is taken too strongly, or repeated too often, it produces a suffocation caused by the weight of the column of air pressing too heavily on the lungs. Therefore, as early as possible, the student should learn to manage his respiration so skillfully, as to reach the end of a long phrase without depriving a single note of its full power and firmness.

STYLE.
Faults to be avoided.

The first matter which calls for the student's special attention is the proper production of the tone. This is the basis of all good execution, and a musician whose method of emission is faulty will never become a great artist.

In the "piano," as well as in the "forte," the "striking," or commencing, of the sound ought to be free, clear and immediate. In striking the tone it is always necessary to articulate the syllable "Tu," and not "Doua," as is the habit of many players. This last-mentioned articulation causes the tone to be flat, and imparts to it a thick and disagreeable quality.

After acquiring the proper methods of tone-production, the player must strive to attain a good style. With this I am not alluding to that supreme quality which represents the culminating point of art, and which is rarely found even among the most skillful and renowned artists, but to a less brilliant quality, the absence of which would check all progress and annihilate all perfection. To be natural, to be correct, to execute music as it is written, to phrase according to the style and sentiment of the piece performed—these are qualities which surely ought to be the object of the pupil's constant endeavors, but he cannot hope to attain them until he has rigorously imposed upon himself the strict observance of the value of each note. The neglect of this desideratum is so common a defect, especially among military bandsmen, that I think it necessary to set forth the evils arising therefrom, and to indicate at the same time the means of avoiding them.

For instance, in a measure (2-4 time) composed of four eighth notes which should be executed with perfect equality by pronouncing:

performers often contrive to prolong the fourth eighth note by pronouncing:

If in this same rhythm a phrase commences with an ascending eighth note, too much

| importance is then given to the first note, which has, in fact, no more value than the others. It should be executed thus, each note being duly separated: | dann dieser Note zu viel Gewicht, welche in der That nicht mehr Werth als die anderen hat. Man muss daher ausführen, indem man jede Note trennt: | alors trop d'importance à cette première note, qui, par le fait, n'a pas plus de valeur que les autres. Il faut exécuter ainsi, en séparant chaque note: |

| instead of prolonging the first note, as follows: | anstatt die erste Note folgendermassen zu verlängern: | au lieu d'allonger la première, ainsi qu'il suit: |

| In 6-8 time the same errors prevail. The sixth eighth note of each bar is prolonged; in fact, the entire six are performed in a skipping and uneven manner. The performer should execute thus: | Im sechs Achtel Takt findet man häufig dasselbe irrige Verfahren. Man verlängert das sechste Achtel eines jeden Taktes, noch glücklich genug, wenn man diese sechs Achtel nicht hüpfend ausführt. Man soll blasen: | Dans la mesure à six-huit, les mêmes errements existent. On allonge la sixième croche de chaque mesure, trop heureux encore quand on n'exécute pas ces six croches en sautillant. On doit exécuter ainsi: |

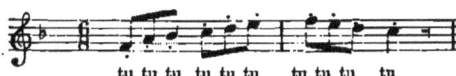

| instead of: | anstatt: | au lieu de: |

| Other players again execute as though there were dotted eighth notes followed by sixteenths: | Andere Künstler machen sogar, als ob es punktirte Achtel mit folgenden Sechszehnteln wären: | D'autres artistes font encore comme s'il y avait des croches pointées suivies de doubles croches: |

From these few remarks alone the reader may readily perceive how much the general execution or style of a player will be influenced by faulty articulation. It must also be borne in mind that the tongue stands in nearly the same relation to brass instruments as the bow to the violin; if you articulate in an unequal manner, you transmit to the notes emitted into the instrument, syllables pronounced in an uneven and irregular manner, together with all the faults of the rhythm resulting therefrom.

In accompaniments, too, there exists a detestable method of playing in contra-tempo. Thus in 3-4 time each note should be performed with perfect equality, without either shortening or prolonging either of the two notes which constitute this kind of accompaniment. For instance:

Der Leser mag aus dem Vorhergehenden ersehen, wie eine schlechte Articulation auf die Ausführung einwirken kann. Man muss sich nicht verhehlen, dass die Zunge bei den Blechinstrumenten nahezu dasselbe ist, was der Bogen bei der Violine; wenn man in ungleicher Weise articulirt, so pflanzt man diese ungleich und hinkend ausgesprochenen Sylben fort auf die Töne, welche man in dem Instrument hervorbringt, zugleich mit den darin enthaltenen rhythmischen Fehlern.

Bei den Accompagnements hat man zuweilen eine abscheuliche Manier, nach zu schlagen. Im 3/4 Takte soll man jede Note mit der grössten Gleichmässigkeit ausführen, ohne eine der beiden Noten, welche diese Art von Begleitung bilden, zu verlängern oder zu verkürzen. Beispiel:

Le lecteur peut voir, par ce qui précède, combien une mauvaise articulation peut influer sur l'exécution; il ne faut pas se dissimuler que la langue étant à peu près aux instruments de cuivre ce que l'archet est au violon, si vous articulez d'une manière inégale, vous transmettez aux notes émises dans l'instrument, les syllabes prononcées d'une façon inégale et boiteuse, et les fautes de rhythme qu'elles contiennent.

Dans les accompagnements, on a aussi, parfois, une manière détestable de faire les contretemps. Ainsi, dans la mesure à trois-quatre, on doit exécuter chaque note avec la plus grande égalité, sans allonger ni raccourcir un des deux notes qui composent ce genre d'accompagnement. Exemple:

| instead of playing, as is often the case: | anstatt, wie man die Gewohnheit hat: | au lieu de faire, comme on en a l'habitude: |

| In 6-8 time there exists an equally faulty method of executing the contra-tempo. This consists in uttering the first note of the contra-tempo as though it were a sixteenth note, instead of imparting the same value to both notes. The performer should execute thus: | Im 6–8 Takt hat man gleichfalls eine schlechte Manier, die Gegentempi auszuführen, nämlich, die erste Note des Gegentempo's hören zu lassen, als wenn sie ein Sechszehntel wäre, anstatt den beiden Noten den gleichen Werth zu geben. Man soll ausführen: | Dans la mesure à six-huit, on a pareillement une mauvaise manière d'exécuter les contretemps, laquelle consiste à faire entendre la première note du contre-temps, comme si c'était une double croche, au lieu de donner la même valeur aux deux notes qui le composent. On doit exécuter ainsi: |

| and not as is indicated in the following example: | und nicht wie das folgende Beispiel zeigt: | et non comme l'indique l'exemple suivant: |

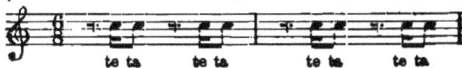

In the execution of syncopated passages there also prevails a radical defect, especially to be found among military bandsmen. It consists in accenting the second half of the sycopated note.

A syncopated passage should be executed by pronouncing:

In der Ausführung der Syncopen giebt es einen Hauptfehler, besonders bei den Regimentsmusikcorps, welcher darin besteht, den zweiten Theil der syncopirten Note merken zu lassen.

Eine Syncope soll hinübergezogen werden, aber man darf die Endung nicht noch mehr hören, als wenn es statt einer Syncope eine Note wäre, die auf dem guten Takttheile angeschlagen wird.

Man muss so ausführen:

Dans l'exécution des syncopes, il existe aussi généralement un défaut capital, surtout dans les régiments, qui consiste à faire sentir la deuxième partie de la note syncopé.

Une syncope doit être traduite, mais il ne faut pas faire entendre sa terminaison davantage que si, au lieu d'être une syncope, c'était une note frappée sur le temps fort.

Il faut l'exécuter en prononçant ainsi:

and not: | und nicht: | et non pas en prononçant::

There is no reason why the middle of a syncope should be performed with greater force than the commencement of the same note. Its essential needs require that the starting point, so to say, should be distinctly heard, and that the note should be sustained throughout its entire value, without increasing its volume toward the middle.

The following illustration must be executed with mechanical equality by pronouncing without pressure:

Es giebt keinen Grund, weshalb die Mitte der Syncope mit mehr Kraft zu Gehör gebracht wird, als der Ansatz derselben Note. Das Wesentlichste ist, den Anfangspunkt bestimmt hören zu lassen, und dieselbe Note während ihres ganzen Werthes auszuhalten, ohne nach der Mitte hin zu schwellen.

Man muss das nachfolgende Beispiel mit einer mechanischen Gleichmässigkeit ausführen, ohne bei der Aussprache zu eilen:

Il n'y a pas de raison pour que le milieu d'une syncope soit entendu avec plus de force que l'attaque de cette même note. L'essentiel consiste à faire entendre distinctement son point de depart, et à soutenir cette même note pendant toute sa valeur, sans l'enfler vers le milieu.

Il faut exécuter l'exemple suivant avec une égalité mécanique, en prononçant sans presser:

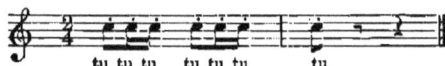

Moreover, it must be observed that the first eighth note should be separated from the two sixteenths, as if a sixteenth rest was placed between them. For instance:

Man muss auch wohl Acht haben, dass das erste Achtel von den beiden folgenden Sechszehnteln getrennt sei, als wenn zwischen ihnen eine Sechszehntheilpause wäre. Beispiel:

observer bien, en outre, que la première croche doit être séparée des deux doubles croches, comme s'il y avait entre elles un quart de soupir. Exemple:

and not, as is often the case, by dragging the first note and producing faulty tonguing as shown herewith:

und nicht, wie gewöhnlich, indem man die erste Note zieht, und einen schlechten Zungenstoss, wie folgt, hervorbringt:

et non pas comme on en a l'habitude, en traînant sur la première note, et en produisant un mauvais coup de langue, ainsi qu'il suit:

Later on the student will learn to perform the same passages with the correct tonguing, but at first the tongue must be trained to express lightly every variety of rhythm, without making use of this kind of articulation.

In addition to the faults of rhythm, just pointed out, there exist many other defects, almost all of which may be attributed to ill-directed ambition, doubtful taste, or lamentable tendency to exaggeration. Many players imagine that they are exhibiting intense feeling when they increase the volume of tones by spasmodic fits and starts, or indulge in a tremolo, produced by means of the neck, a practice which results in an "Ou, ou, ou" of a most disagreeable nature.

The oscillation of a sound is obtained on the cornet, as on the violin, by a slight movement of the right hand; the result is highly sensitive and effective, but care must be taken not to indulge in this practice too freely, as its too frequent employment becomes a serious defect.

Später wird man die Art und Weise lernen, dieselben Phrasen im Zungenstoss auszuführen, doch muss man vorläufig die Zunge üben, jede Gattung von Takt mit Leichtigkeit auszusprechen, ohne zu dieser Art der Articulation seine Zuflucht zu nehmen.

Ausser den bereits bezeichneten rhythmischen Fehlern giebt es noch viele andere Fehler, die fast alle ihren Grund in einem falschen Ehrgeize, in einem schwankenden Geschmacke oder in einem leidigen Hange zur Uebertreibung haben. Manche Künstler bilden sich ein, dass sie ein Zeichen des Gefühls von sich geben, wenn sie die Töne haben ruckweise anschwellen lassen, und wenn sie ein vermöge des Halses hervorgebrachtes Zittern missbraucht haben, das ein gewisses unangenehmes u, u, u vernehmen lässt.

Das Beben des Tons erhält man bei dem Cornet à pistons auf dieselbe Weise, wie bei der Violine, durch eine leichte Bewegung der rechten Hand. Dieses Effectmittel ist sehr ausdrucksvoll, aber man muss sich hüten, dasselbe zu missbrauchen, denn eine zu häufige Anwendung würde ein grober Fehler sein.

Plus tard, vous apprendrez la manière d'exécuter les mêmes traits en coup de langue, mais il faut préalablement exercer la langue à prononcer avec beaucoup de légèreté toute espèce de rhythme sans avoir recours à ce genre d'articulation.

En dehors des défauts de rhythme qui viennent d'être signalés, il existe beaucoup d'autres défauts; presque tous peuvent se rapporter à une ambition mal dirigée, à un goût douteux, à une fâcheuse tendance aux exagérations. Bien des artistes se figurent qu'ils font preuve de sentiment quand ils ont enflé des sons par saccade, et qu'ils ont abusé d'un tremblement produit au moyen du cou, et qui laisse entendre un certain ou ou ou des plus désagréables.

L'oscillation du son s'obtient sur le cornet, de la même manière que sur le violon, par un léger mouvement de la main droite; ce genre d'effet produit une grande sensibilité, mais il faut se garder d'en faire abus, car son emploi trop fréquent deviendrait un grave défaut.

The same observation applies to the portamento preceded by an appoggiatura. Some players are unable to execute four consecutive notes without introducing one or two portamenti. This is a very reprehensible habit, which, together with the abuse of the gruppetto, should be carefully avoided.

Before terminating this chapter, wherein I have passed in review the most salient and striking defects engendered by a faulty style (duly pointing out, at the same time, the means of remedying the same), I pledge myself to return to the subject whenever occasion for doing so may present itself. Wrong habits are, in general, too deeply rooted in performers on brass instruments to yield to a single warning, and therefore require vigorous and constant correction.

Dieselbe Beobachtung gilt für das Portamento mit vorangehendem Vorschlag; es giebt Künstler, welche nicht vier Noten ausführen können, ohne ein oder zwei Portamento's anzubringen. Diese Manier muss als ebenso bedauerlich bezeichnet werden, wie der Missbrauch des Gruppetto.

Indem ich diesen Paragraphen beschliesse, in welchem ich die hervorragendsten und häufigsten Fehler, die einen schlechten Styl verursachen (indem ich die Art und Weise, ihnen abzuhelfen, angegeben), anführte, mache ich es mir zur Pflicht, mit Hartnäckigkeit jedes Mal, wenn sich Gelegenheit dazu bietet, auf diesen Gegenstand zurückzukommen. Die schlechten Angewohnheiten sind im Allgemeinen bei den Musikern der Blechinstrumente zu tief eingewurzelt, um einer einzigen Erinnerung zu weichen, und man wird sie daher niemals strenge genug bekämpfen können.

Même observation en ce qui concerne le *portamento* précédé d'une petite note; il y a des artistes qui ne peuvent pas faire quatre notes sans y introduire un ou deux *portamento*; c'est là une manière déplorable qu'il convient de signaler, ainsi que l'abus du gruppetto.

En terminant le paragraphe où j'ai passé en revue les défauts les plus saillants et les plus fréquents qu'engendre un mauvais style (en indiquant la manière d'y remédier), je prends l'engagement de revenir avec insistance sur ce sujet chaque fois que s'en présentera l'occasion. Les mauvaises habitudes sont généralement trop enracinées chez les musiciens qui jouent des instruments de cuivre, pour céder à un seul avertissement, et on ne saurait leur faire une assez rude guerre.

Explanatory Comments on The First Studies.

No. 1. Commence or "strike" the sound by pronouncing the syllable "Tu;" sustain it well, and at the same time impart to it all possible strength and brilliancy.

Under no circumstances should the cheeks ever be puffed out; the lips should make no noise in the mouthpiece, though many performers appear to think otherwise. The sound forms itself; it should be well "struck," by a proper tension of the lips, so that it may be properly in tune, and not below its diapason, for in the latter case a disagreeable and untuneful sound would be the result.

Nos. 7 and 8 indicate all the notes which are produced by employing the same valves. Nos. 9 and 10, passing as they do through all the keys, are destined to complete the subject of fingering, so that hereafter I shall not consider it necessary to mark the numbers of the valves under each note. The first two lessons should therefore be practiced for a considerable period, in order that the student may be perfectly at home as regards the fingering of the instrument.

Therefore, from now on, I shall only mark the fingering in passages where same will facilitate matters. Throughout all the lessons, up to No. 50, it will be necessary to strike each sound, and give to each note its exact value, these studies having been composed with this special end in view.

Erklärungen über die ersten Etuden.

No. 1. Man setze den Ton an, indem man die Sylbe *tü* ausspricht, halte ihn gut aus, und gebe ihm dabei möglichsten Glanz und möglichste Stärke.

Man darf unter keiner Bedingung die Backen aufblasen; die Lippen sollen kein Geräusch in dem Mundstück machen, wie Viele es sich einbilden. Der Ton bildet sich aus sich selbst; man muss ihn nur gut ansetzen, indem man die Lippen spannt, damit er auf seiner Höhe, und nicht unter der Stimmung ist, denn daraus würde ein unangenehmer und falscher Ton entstehen.

No. 7 und 8 zeigen die Noten, welche sich bei Anwendung derselben Pistons bilden. No. 9 und 10, übergehend in alle Tonarten, sind dazu bestimmt, das Zusammenwirken der Fingersätze zu vervollkommen, der Art, dass man nicht mehr nöthig hat, die Nummern der Pistons bei jeder Note zu bemerken. Man muss jedoch die beiden ersten Lectionen ziemlich lange üben, um mit dem Fingersatze vollständig vertraut zu werden.

Ich werde künftighin nur die Fingersätze anführen, welche Erleichterung gewähren. In allen Lectionen bis zu No. 50 muss man beständig jeden Ton ansetzen, und jeder Note ihren wirklichen Werth geben; alle ersten Etuden sind in dieser Absicht componirt.

Explication sur les premières études.

No. 1. Attaquez le son en prononçant la syllabe *tu*, et soutenez-le bien en lui donnant tout l'éclat et toute la force possibles.

On ne doit, en aucune circonstance, gonfler les joues; les lèvres ne doivent faire aucun bruit dans l'embouchure, ainsi que beaucoup de personnes se le figurent. Le son se forme de lui-même; on doit seulement le bien attaquer, en tendant les lèvres, afin qu'il soit à sa hauteur et non pas au-dessous de son diapason, car, alors, il en résulterait un son désagréable et faux.

Les numéros 7 et 8 indiquent toutes les notes qui se font en employant les mêmes pistons. Les numéros 9 et 10, en passant dans tous les tons, sont destinés à compléter l'ensemble des doigtés, de manière à ne plus être obligé de marquer les numéros de pistons sous chaque note. Il faut donc jouer les deux premières leçons pendant assez longtemps, pour être bien au courant du doigté de l'instrument.

Je n'indiquerai désormais que les doigtés qui donnent quelques facilités. Dans toutes les leçons jusqu'au no. 50, il faut constamment attaquer chaque son et donner à chaque note leurs valeurs véritables; toutes les premières études sont composées dans ce but.

Syncopated Passages.

Syncopation occurs when the accent falls upon the light, instead of the heavy, beat of a measure. The accented note must be sustained throughout its full value, the commencement of the note being duly marked, but the second half of the duration of a note should never be disjointly uttered.

A passage of this kind should be executed as follows:

Von den Syncopen.

Die Syncope ist eine Note, welche, anstatt auf dem guten, auf dem schlechten Takttheil steht. Man muss sie während der ganzen Dauer ihres Werthes halten, und ihren Ausgangspunkt gut merken lassen; in keinem Falle darf man aber durch einen Ruck den zweiten Theil des Werthes zu Gehör bringen.

Man muss ausführen:

Des Syncopes.

La syncope est une note qui, au lieu d'être placée sur le temps fort, se place sur le temps faible. On doit la soutenir pendant toute la durée de sa valeur, en faisant bien sentir son point de départ; mais il ne faut, en aucun cas faire entendre par saccade la deuxième partie de sa valeur.

On doit exécuter ainsi:

and not: | und nicht: | et non pas ainsi:

Studies in Dotted Eighth Notes Followed by Sixteenths.

Etuden in punktirten Achteln mit folgenden Sechszehnteln.

Études en croches pointées suivies de doubles croches.

In these studies the eighth note should be sustained throughout its entire value; care must be taken never to substitute a rest for the dot.

The performer should play:

In diesen Etuden muss das punktirte Achtel während seines ganzen Werthes ausgehalten werden; man muss sich hüten, den Punkt durch eine Pause zu ersetzen.

Man muss ausführen:

Dans ces études, la croche pointée doit être soutenue pendant toute sa valeur; il faut se garder de remplacer le point par un silence.

On doit exécuter ainsi:

and not as though it were written: | und nicht: | et non pas comme s'il y avait:

Studies Consisting of Eighth Notes Followed by Sixteenths.

Etuden von Achteln mit folgenden Sechszehnteln.

Études composées de croches suivies de doubles croches.

In order to impart lightness to these studies, the first eighth note should be played in a shorter manner than its value would seem to indicate. It should be executed like a sixteenth note, a rest being introduced between it and the two sixteenths which follow it. The passage is written:

Um diesen Etuden mehr Leichtigkeit zu geben, muss man das erste Achtel etwas kürzer nehmen, als sein Werth ist; man muss es wie ein Sechzehntel ausführen, indem man zwischen dem Achtel und den beiden folgenden Sechszehnteln eine Pause macht.

Schreibart:

Pour donner plus de légèreté à ces études, il faut que la première croche soit attaquée avec plus de sécheresse que ne l'indique sa valeur; on doit l'exécuter comme une double croche, en observant un silence entre elle et les deux doubles croches qui la suivent.

On écrit ainsi:

and should be played thus: | Ausführung: | et l'on doit exécuter ainsi:

The same remark applies to an eighth note following, instead of preceding, the sixteenth.

Written:

Ebenso ist es auch, wenn ein Achtel, anstatt voranzugehen, den Sechszehnteln folgt:

Schreibart:

Il en est de même quand une croche, au lieu de précéder, suit les doubles croches.

On écrit ainsi:

should be played thus: | Ausführung: | et l'on doit exécuter ainsi:

Written: | Schreibart: | On écrit ainsi:

should be executed thus: | Ausführung: | et l'on doit exécuter ainsi:

Studies in 6/8 Time.

Etuden über den 6/8 Takt.

Études sur la mesure à 6/8

In 6-8 time, the eighth notes should be well separated, and should have equal value allotted to them. Consequently, the third eighth note in each measure should never be dragged. Dotted eighths and eighths followed by sixteenths are played in this rhythm, by observing the same rules as in 2-4 time.

Im 6-8 Takte muss man die Achtel ausführen, indem man sie wohl trennt und ihnen einen gleichen Werth giebt. Man muss also niemals auf dem dritten Achtel ziehen. Die punktirten Achtel, wie die Achtel mit folgenden Sechszehnteln werden in diesem Takt, unter denselben Regeln, wie im 2–4 Takt ausgeführt.

Dans la mesure à 6-8, on doit exécuter les croches en les séparant bien et en leur donnant une valeur égale. Il ne faut en conséquence jamais traîner sur la troisième croche de chaque temps. Les croches pointées, ainsi que les croches suivies de doubles croches, s'exécutent dans ce rhythme, en observant les mêmes règles que dans le 2-4.

FIRST STUDIES.   ERSTE ETUDEN.   PREMIÈRES ETUDES.

12

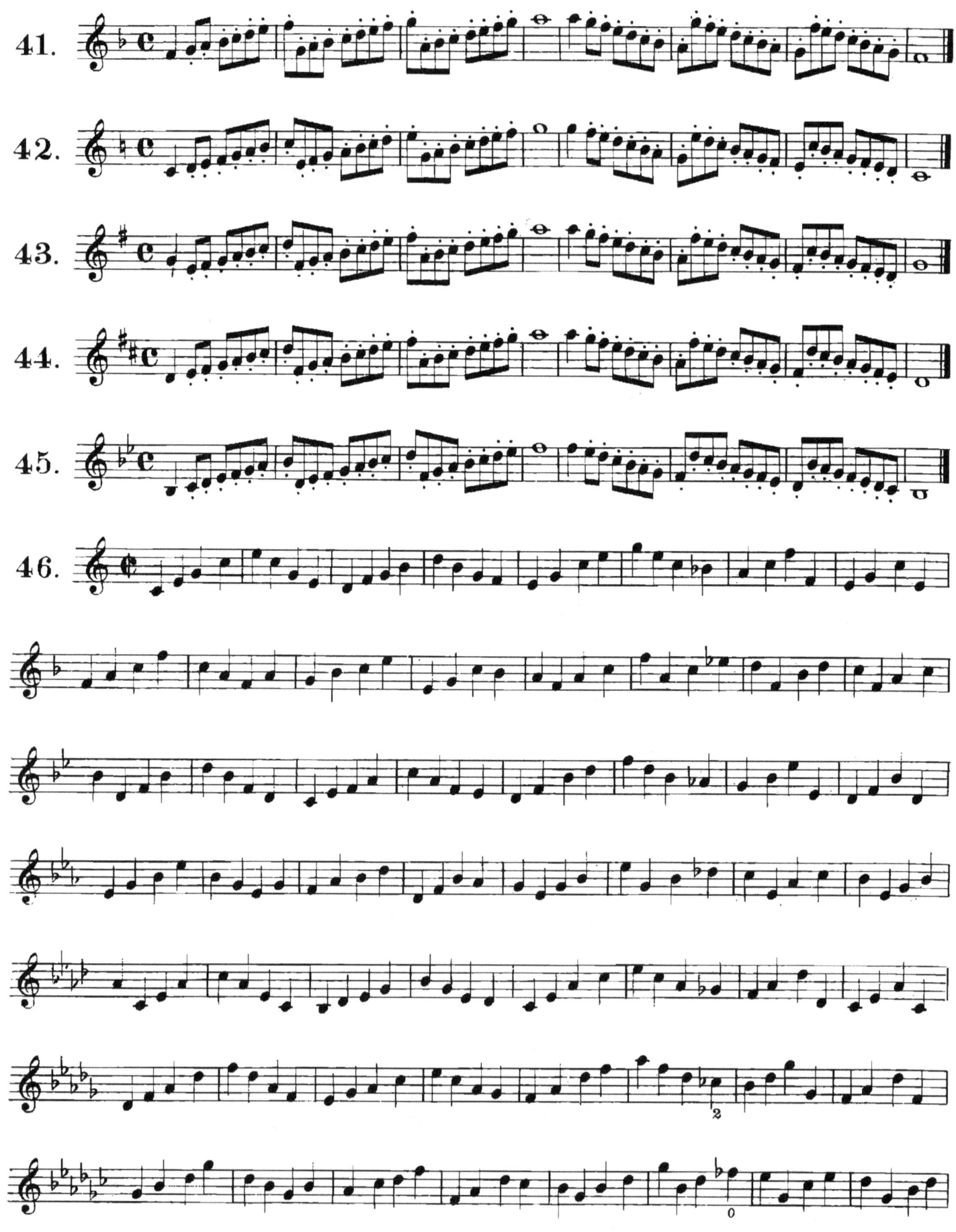

47.

STUDIES ON SYNCOPATION. | *STUDIEN ÜBER DIE SYNCOPEN.* | ÉTUDES SUR LES SYNCOPES.

Studies on dotted eighth notes followed by sixteenths. | Etuden über die punktirten Achtel mit folgenden Sechszehnteln. | Études sur les croches pointées suivies de doubles croches.

Tempo di Marcia.

13.

Allegro moderato.

14.

Allegro.

15.

EXPLANATION
for the Studies on the Slur.

Without question this is one of the most important portions of my method, and I have devoted considerable space to its exposition. Particular attention has been given to those exercises which are produced by movements of the lips alone, without the aid or substitution of a valve. The fingering must be used exactly as indicated, no matter how unusual it may appear. I have purposely indicated the fingering as I did, not because I wished to recommend its habitual usage, but in order to invest this kind of exercise with unusual difficulties through which the lips are compelled to move and produce the notes without the aid of valves.

This exercise, moreover, is analogous to that practiced by singers when they study the movement of the glottis in order to master the trill.

The easiest interval to perform in this manner is that of the minor second. The interval of the major second is somewhat more difficult, as a certain movement of the lips is necessary in order to obtain it.

The interval of the third is the most difficult of all, for it is often met with in situations wherein it becomes impossible to have recourse to the valves to assist in carrying the sound from the lower, to the higher note.

I therefore recommend the diligent practice of this kind of exercise; it becomes the foundation of an easy and brilliant execution. It imparts great suppleness to the lips, and is an essential aid for mastering the trill.

Trilling through means of the lips alone is only desirable for intervals of a second, as in Exercise No. 23, and then only if the indicated fingering is employed; otherwise trills in thirds will result, and these are both annoying and objectionable.

I merely suggest these exercises as studies and in no way do I advise pupils to adopt them in general practice, as is the case with certain players who wish to apply to the cornet a system which has no solid foundation. The cornet is one of the most complete and perfect of all instruments and repudiates rather than requires all factitious practices, the effect of which will always appear detestable to people of taste.

I must take this opportunity of pointing out an intolerable defect, much affected by the adepts of this school, as regards the movement of the lips; I allude to the manner in which they execute the gruppetto.

In order to execute this ornament on the cornet, all that is required is the regular movement of the fingers, and each note will be emitted with irreproachable precision and purity.

ERKLÄRUNG
der Etuden über das Schleifen.

Dieser Theil der Schule ist unstreitig einer der wichtigsten; ich habe ihm daher eine grosse Ausdehnung eingeräumt, besonders in den Uebungen, welche speciell durch die Lippenbewegung gemacht werden, d.h. ohne die Hinzuziehung oder Substituirung eines Pistons. Man muss dem angezeigten Fingersatze folgen, wenn er auch ungebraüchlich ist. Ich habe diese Fingersätze zu Hülfe genommen, nicht etwa, um ihren Gebrauch in der gewöhnlichen Ausführung anzuempfehlen, sondern vielmehr, um dieser Gattung von Uebungen eine Schwierigkeit zu verleihen, die um jeden Preis zu überwinden ist, mit andern worten: um die Lippen zu zwingen, sich zu bewegen, ohne zur Anwendung der Pistons seine Zuflucht zu nehmen.

Diese Uebung ist übrigens verwandt mit der, welche die Sänger ausführen, wenn sie die Bewegung der Stimmritze üben um zu dem Triller zu gelangen.

Das leichteste Intervall zum Schleifen ist das Intervall der kleinen Seconde, das Intervall der grossen Seconde ist ein wenig schwerer, denn man muss schon eine gewisse Bewegung der Lippen anwenden, um es zu erhalten.

Das Intervall einer Terz ist das schwerste, denn es befindet sich oft auf Stufen, wo es unmöglich wird, die Pistons zu Hülfe zu nehmen, um den Ton der tiefen Note zu der hohen Note hinaufzuziehen.

Ich rathe an, diese Art von Uebungen emsig zu studiren; sie wird die Quelle einer leichten und brillanten Ausführung; man erhält durch sie eine grosse Geschmeidigkeit der Lippen, besonders wenn man die Ausführung des Trillers erreichen will.

Der Triller vermittelst der Lippen ist nur für die Intervalle gut, in denen die Töne eine Seconde von einander liegen, wie in der Uebung No. 23, und besonders, wenn man dem angezeigten Fingersatze folgt, sonst würde man Terztriller machen, die ebenso unangenehm, als schlecht sind.

Ich stelle diese Uebungen nur als Studien hin, und verpflichte die Schüler keineswegs, sich ihrer in der Praxis zu bedienen, wie es manche Hornisten thun, die dem Cornet à pistons ein System anhängen, welches durchaus keine Berechtigung hat denn dies Instrument ist eines der vollkommensten und vollständigsten, welches erkünstelte Proceduren, deren Effect Leuten von Geschmack abscheulich sein muss, eher verwirft, als verlangt.

Ich muss bei dieser Gelegenheit noch einen unerträglichen Fehler bezeichnen, den die Anhänger dieser Schule zu lieben scheinen einen Fehler vermittelst der Bewegung der Lippen. Ich will von der Art sprechen, wie sie den Gruppetto machen.

Um diese Verzierung auf dem Cornet à Pistons auszuführen, genügt es, die Finger regelmässig zu bewegen, und jede Note kommt mit einer untadelhaften Bestimmtheit und Reinheit heraus.

EXPLICATION
des Etudes sur le coule.

Cette partie de la méthode est sans condredit une des plus importantes; aussi lui ai-je donné un grand développement, surtout dans les exercices qui se font spécialement par le mouvement des lèvres c'est à-dire sans avoir recours à l'addition ou à la substitution d'un piston. On devra suivre exactement les doigtés indiqués, quoique étant inusités. C'est à dessein, en effet, que j'ai eu recours à ces doigtés, non plus pour en conseiller l'usage dans l'exécution habituelle, mais afin de donner à ce genre d'exercice une difficulté qui doit absolument être surmontée, autrement dit, en obligeant les lèvres à se mouvoir, sans avoir recours à l'emploi des pistons.

Ce travail est, du reste, analogue à celui auquel se livrent les chanteurs quand ils étudient le mouvement de la glotte pour arriver à faire le trille.

L'intervalle le plus facile à couler est l'intervalle de seconde mineure; l'intervalle de seconde majeure est un peu plus difficile, car il faut déjà faire un certain mouvement des lèvres pour l'obtenir.

L'intervalle de tierce est le plus difficile, car il se trouve souvent sur des degrés où il devient impossible d'avoir recours aux pistons pour aider à porter le son de la note basse sur la note haute.

Je conseille donc de travailler assidûment ce genre d'exercice; il devient la source d'une exécution facile et brillante; on obtient par lui une grande souplesse de lèvres, surtout quand on peut arriver jusqu'à l'exécution du trille.

Le trille, au moyen des lèvres, n'est bon que pour les intervalles où les harmoniques sont à distance de seconde, comme dans l'exercice no. 23, et surtout en suivant les doigtés indiqués, autrement on ferait des trilles de tierces qui seraient aussi désagréables que mauvais.

Je ne donne donc ces exercices que comme études, et je n'engage aucunement les élèves à s'en servir dans la pratique, ainsi que le font certains cornistes qui veulent appliquer au cornet à pistons un système qui n'a aucune raison d'être, puisque c'est un instrument des plus parfaits et des plus complets qui répudie plutôt qu'il n'exige des procédés factices dont l'effet paraîtra toujours détestable aux gens de goût.

Je dois signaler encore à ce propos un vice intolérable que semblent affectionner les adeptes de cette école, par le mouvement des lèvres. Je veux parler de la manière dont ils font le gruppetto.

Pour exécuter cet ornement sur le cornet à pistons, il suffit de remuer régulièrement les doigts, et chaque note sort avec une justesse et une pureté irréprochables.

By what right, then, do certain performers substitute an upper third for the appoggiatura which ought only to be an interval of a second? Why, in short, do they play:

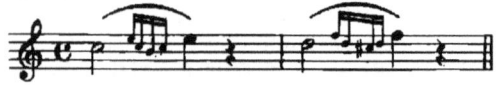

instead of playing:

which is the only correct method; and why is this done on all the different degrees of the scale? The answer is that these gentlemen find it more convenient to have recourse to a simple movement of the lips, which obviates the necessity of moving their fingers; as though it were not more natural to emit the true notes by employing the valves.

Some performers pursue this evil practice still farther, and do not hesitate to execute triplet passages with the movement of the lips, instead of having recourse to the valves.

Illustration from a study by Mr. Gallay:

The passage with aid of the valves, should be executed thus:

instead of merely employing the lips, which would result in the following execrable effect:

I need insist no farther to point out that such sleight-of-hand tricks are totally out of place on the cornet, and if I mention them here at all, it is merely to put the pupil on his guard against a system which, unfortunately is entirely too prevalent among performers in military bands.

The principal object of the first fifteen numbers of this division is to instruct the pupil in the so-called *portamento* effects. In order to arrive at this result, the lower note must be slightly inflated, and when it has reached the extremity of its power, it must be slurred up to the higher note by a slight pressure of the mouthpiece on the lips.

Then follows the practicing of thirds which is obtained by the tension of the muscles, and also by the pressure of the mouthpiece on the lips. The notes should be produced with perfect equality; they must be connected with each other with absolute evenness, and played precisely according to the time and with the exact fingering as indicated.

The studies, Nos. 16 to 69, were composed for the sole purpose of teaching how to play thirds in this way and to enable the student to execute the little grace notes and double appoggiaturas with the necessary facility and elegance. A few examples of this kind have been added to this series of studies, although their more thorough treatment occurs at a later period, when taking up the study of grace notes in detail.

As the above embellishments are solely produced through lip-movements, I have thought it advisable to offer a few illustrations of same herewith.

Mit welchem Recht nun ersetzen manche Künstler die Appoggiatur durch eine grosse Terze, da sie doch nur eine Seconde sein soll? Warum, mit einem Worte, blasen sie:

anstatt zu blasen:

welches die einzige richtige Art und Weise ist – und warum dies auf allen Stufen der Tonleiter? Weil diese Herren es bequemer finden, eine einfache Lippenbewegung anzuwenden, welche sie der Bewegung der Finger überhebt; als ob es nicht natürlicher wäre, die richtigen Noten mit Anwendung der Pistons zu blasen.

In dieser Hinsicht gehen Einige noch weiter, und nehmen keinen Anstand, Triolenfolgen vermittelst der Lippenbewegung auszuführen, anstatt die Pistons zu Hülfe zu nehmen.

Beispiel einer Etude von Gallay:

Man soll mit Anwendung der Pistons ausführen:

anstatt das Lippenspiel anzuwenden, welches folgende abscheuliche Wirkung hervorbringt:

Ich habe nicht nöthig, noch weiter zu zeigen, dass derartige Kunststücke auf dem Cornet à pistons keine Berechtigung haben, und wenn ich ihrer hier erwähne, so geschieht es nur, um den Schüler zur Vorsicht zu mahnen einem Systeme gegenüber, das leider in der Armee nur zu verbreitet ist.

Die ersten 15 Nummern dieses Theiles sind einzig und allein da, um das Hinüberziehen des Tons zu lernen. Man muss, um zu diesem Ziele zu gelangen, die tiefe Note ein wenig anblasen, und sie, im Moment, wo ihre Stärke den Gipfel erreicht, zur hohen Note hinaufziehen vermittelst eines leichten Druckes, den das Mundstück auf die Lippen ausübt.

Man gehe sodann zur Uebung des Terzintervalles über, welches sich durch die Spannung der Muskeln und auch durch den Druck, welchen das Mundstück auf die Lippen ausübt, ergiebt. Man spreche jede Note gleichmässig aus, verbinde sie unter einander wohl und befolge Zeitmass und angezeigten Fingersatz.

Alle Etuden, von 16 bis 69 sind einzig und allein componirt, um zu lernen, wie man die Terzintervalle mit Leichtigkeit hinüberzieht, damit man die kleinen geschleiften Noten und die Doppelappoggiaturen mit Eleganz ausführen kann, — wovon ich schon in dieser Reihe von Etuden einige Beispiele angeführt habe, — die ich aber erst später bei dem Artikel über die Verzierungsnoten ausführlich behandeln werde.

Da diese beiden Verzierungen nur durch die Lippenbewegung zu erhalten sind, so glaubte ich darüber hier einige Anwendungen geben zu müssen.

De quel droit alors certains artistes remplacent-ils par une tierce supérieure l'appoggiatura qui doit être à distance de seconde? Pourquoi, en un mot, exécutent-ils:

qui est la seule manière convenable – et cela sur tous les degrés de la gamme? parce que ces Messieurs trouvent plus commode de recourir à un simple mouvement des lèvres qui les dispense de remuer les doigts; comme s'il n'était pas plus naturel de faire sortir les vraies notes en employant les pistons.

Dans cette voie, quelques-uns vont plus loin encore et n'hésitent pas à exécuter des successions de triolet par le mouvement des lèvres, au lieu de recourir aux pistons.

Exemple d'une étude de M. Gallay:

On doit exécuter ainsi, en employant les pistons:

au lieu d'employer le jeu de lèvres, ce qui produit l'exécrable effet suivant:

Je n'ai pas besoin d'insister davantage pour faire voir que de pareils escamotages n'ont aucune raison d'être sur le cornet à pistons, et si j'en fais mention ici, ce n'est que pour mettre l'élève en garde contre un système malheureusement trop répandu dans l'armée.

Les quinze premiers neméros de cette partie ont uniquement pour object d'apprendre à porter le son. Il faut, pour arriver à ce résultat, enfler un peu la note grave, et, au moment où elle arrive à l'apogée de sa force, la porter sur la note haute par le moyen d'une légère pression de l'embouchure sur les lèvres.

Arrive ensuite le travail de l'intervalle de tierce, qui s'obtient par la tension des muscles et aussi par la pression de l'embouchure sur les lèvres. Faites parler chaque note avec beaucoup d'egalité en les liant bien entre elles et en suivant les rhythmes et les doigtés indiqués.

Toutes les études, à partir du no. 16 jusqu'au no. 69, sont uniquement composées pour apprendre à porter avec facilité les intervalles de tierces, afin d'arriver à passer avec élégance les petites notes portées, ainsi que les doubles appoggiatures, — dont j'ai déjà ajouté quelques exemples à cette série d'études, — mais qui plus tard, seront traitées fond à l'article des notes d'agrément.

Ces deux agréments ne s'obtenant que par le mouvement des lèvres, j'ai cru devoir en donner ici quelques applications.

Studies on the Slur (or Legato.) Studien über das Schleifen. Études sur le Coulé.

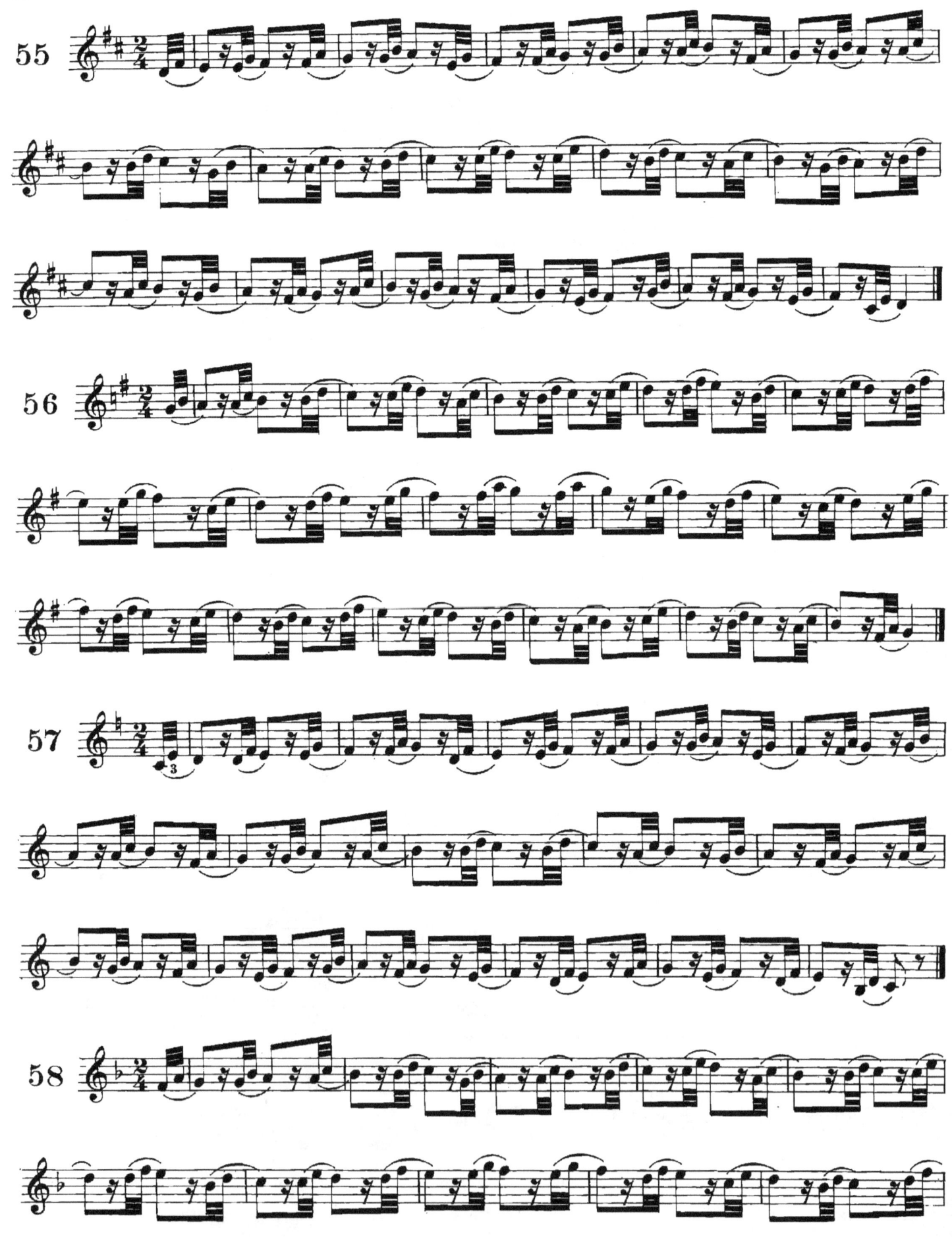

Allegro.

63.

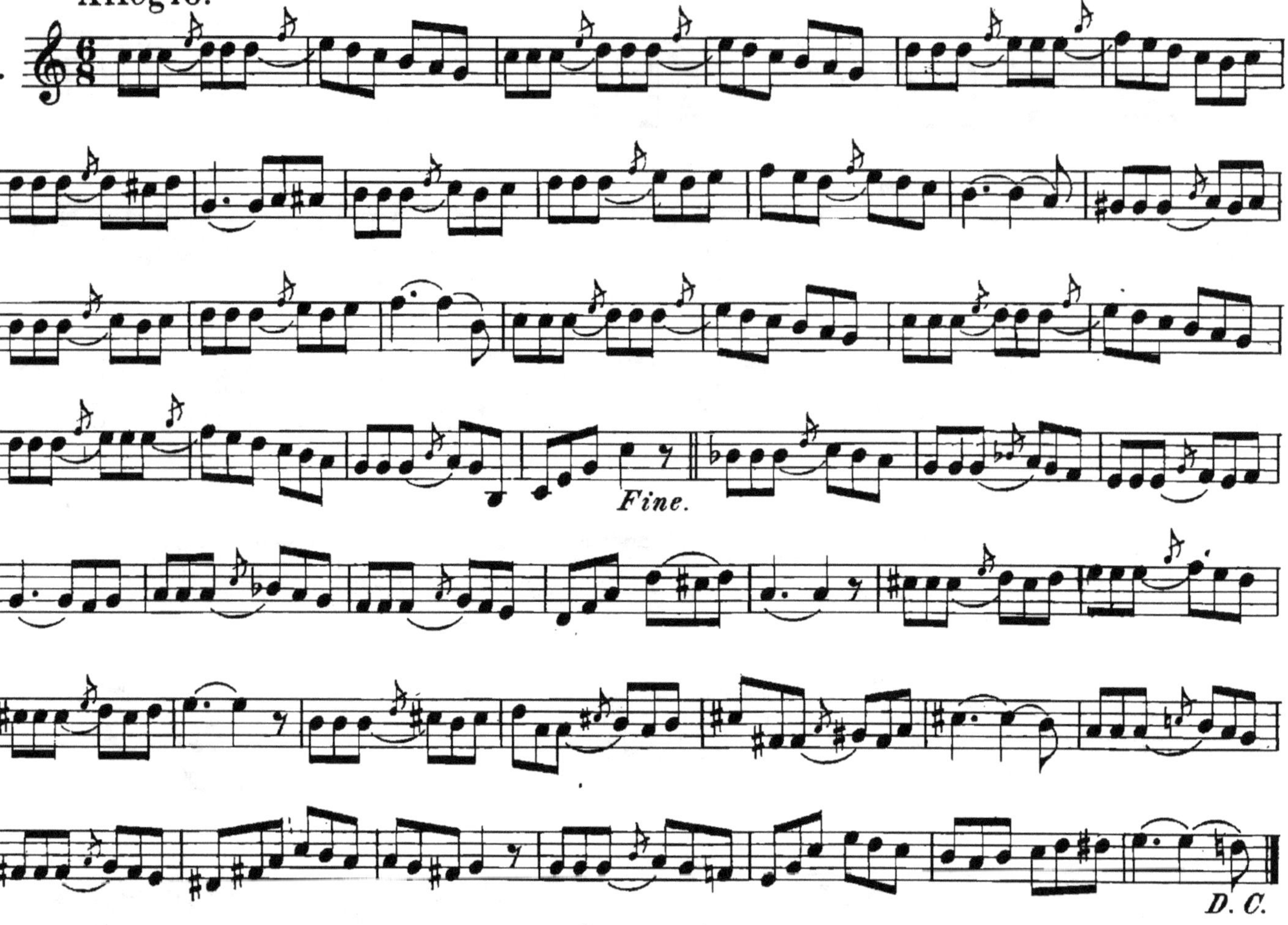

64.

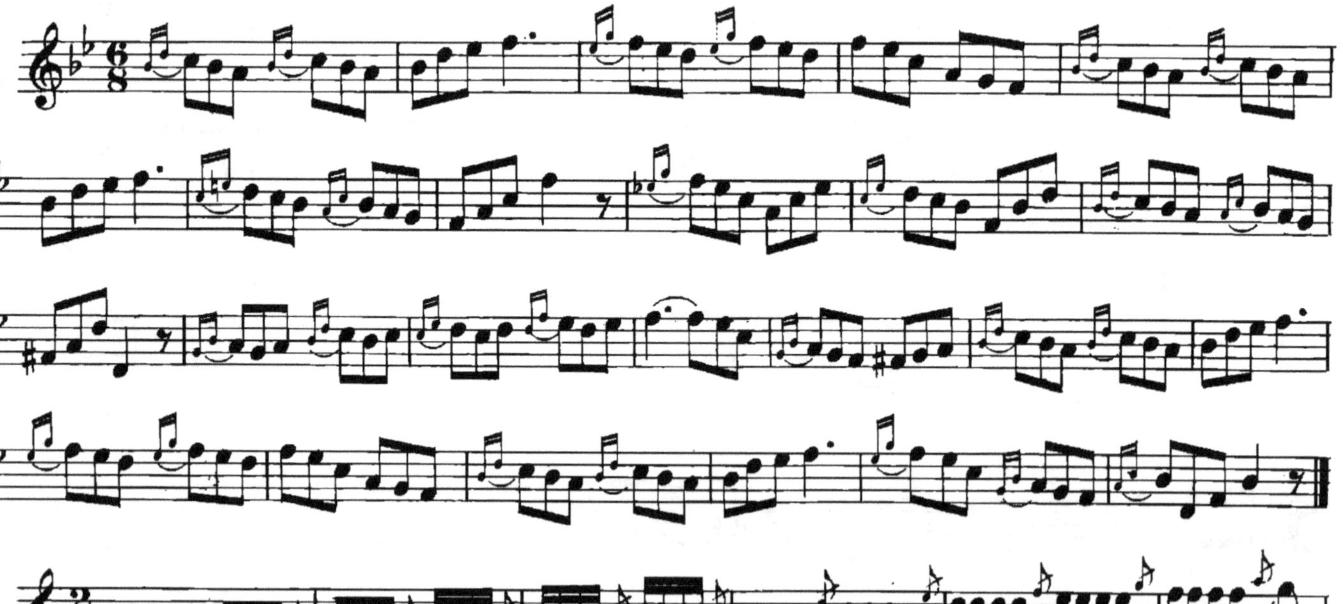

65.

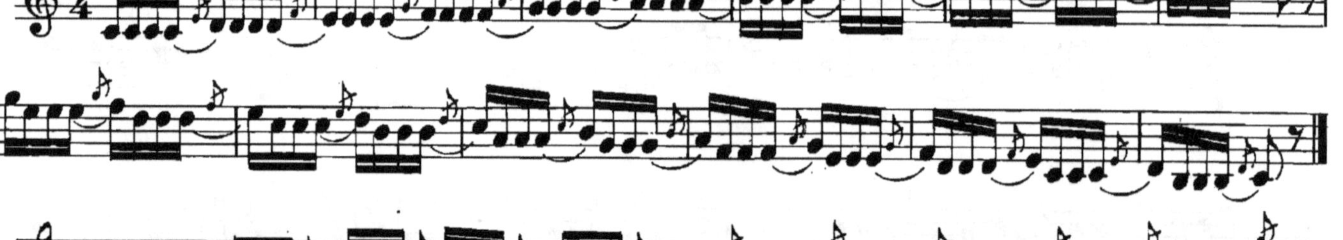

66.

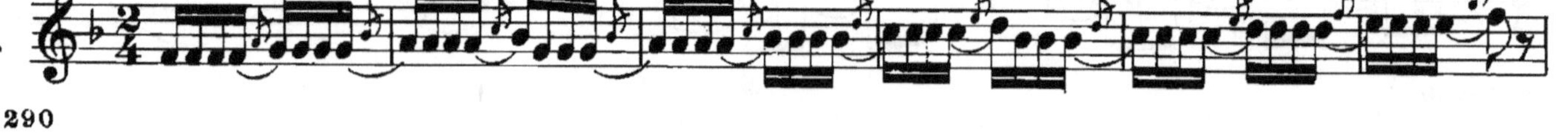

www.ingramcontent.com/pod-product-compliance
Lightning Source LLC
Chambersburg PA
CBHW081828170426
43202CB00019B/2980

Réimpression de la plus connue et plus répandue partout dans l'école du monde pour trompette et autres cuivres par Jean-Baptiste ARBAN.
Ce livre contient le premier volume complet.

Trait Biographique de la vie de Joseph-Jean-Baptiste-Laurent Arban

Ce célébre musicien est né a Lyon en France, le 28-me Fevrier, 1825. Il fut élève du Conservatoire encore jeune, pour étudier la trompette sous Daverné, et obtint le premier prix en 1845. Son devoir militaire fut passé dans la marine sur "La Belle Poule" donc le chef de musique, Paulus, devint chef de musique de la Garde à Paris pendant le reigne de Napoleon III.

Après avoir étè professeur de la classe de saxhorn a l'école militaire (1857) il fut nommé professeur d'une classe de cornet au Conservatoire le 23-me Janvier, 1869. Après qu'il s'était devoué à ces devoirs pendant une période de cinque ans, Arban quitta le Conservatoire pour six ans, retournant de nouveau en 1880.

Il était le plus brillant cornettiste de son jour et son jeu étonnant, ainsi que les triomphes que lui accordait toute l'Europe pendant ses tournées de concerts, furent le moyen d'etablir le cornet à pistons comme un des plus populaires d'instruments musicale. Arban a perpetué son ideal d'Art, son profond savoir musical, et ses remarquables principes instructifs dans son excellente Methode pour le Cornet qui retient encore le premier rang parmi les oeuvres instructifs de mêne genre, et n'a jamais été surpassée au point de superiorité pratique ou de plan artistique.

Arban mourut a Paris le 9-me Avril, 1889. Il était un officier de l'Académie, Chevalier de l'Ordre de Leopold de Belge, de Christ de
Portugal, d'Isabelle la Catholique, et de la Croix Russe.

Europäischer Musikverlag

9783956980879

ISBN 978-3-95698-087-9

JEAN-BAPTISTE ARBAN

ARBAN'S COMPLETE CELEBRATED METHOD FOR THE CORNET

TRUMPET, BUGLE AND OTHERS

VOLUME 1

Europäischer Musikverlag